50 Cinnamon Sensation Recipes for Home

By: Kelly Johnson

Table of Contents

- Cinnamon Apple Pancakes
- Cinnamon Sugar Pull-Apart Bread
- Cinnamon Rolls with Cream Cheese Frosting
- Cinnamon Apple Pie
- Cinnamon Swirl Coffee Cake
- Cinnamon Raisin Bread
- Cinnamon French Toast
- Cinnamon Pecan Sticky Buns
- Cinnamon Pear Crisp
- Cinnamon Almond Granola
- Cinnamon Spice Cake
- Cinnamon Banana Bread
- Cinnamon Pumpkin Muffins
- Cinnamon Apple Crumble Bars
- Cinnamon Ginger Cookies
- Cinnamon Honey Butter
- Cinnamon Peach Cobbler
- Cinnamon Oatmeal Raisin Cookies
- Cinnamon Chocolate Chip Scones
- Cinnamon Maple Glazed Carrots
- Cinnamon Cranberry Sauce
- Cinnamon Vanilla Rice Pudding
- Cinnamon Sweet Potato Casserole
- Cinnamon Hazelnut Latte
- Cinnamon Cherry Jam
- Cinnamon Coconut Macaroons
- Cinnamon Lemonade
- Cinnamon Apricot Chutney
- Cinnamon Whipped Cream
- Cinnamon Plum Tart
- Cinnamon Pistachio Biscotti
- Cinnamon Orange Rolls
- Cinnamon Mint Tea
- Cinnamon Pineapple Upside-Down Cake
- Cinnamon Mocha Brownies

- Cinnamon Raspberry Smoothie
- Cinnamon Steak Rub
- Cinnamon Pesto Pasta
- Cinnamon Chicken Curry
- Cinnamon Lentil Soup
- Cinnamon Garlic Shrimp
- Cinnamon Lamb Kebabs
- Cinnamon Chili
- Cinnamon Cornbread Stuffing
- Cinnamon Bacon Wrapped Dates
- Cinnamon BBQ Sauce
- Cinnamon Sweet Chili Wings
- Cinnamon Avocado Toast
- Cinnamon Spinach Salad
- Cinnamon Sourdough Bread

Cinnamon Apple Pancakes

Ingredients:

- 1 cup all-purpose flour
- 2 tbsp sugar
- 1 tsp baking powder
- 1/2 tsp baking soda
- 1/2 tsp salt
- 1 tsp ground cinnamon
- 1 cup buttermilk
- 1 egg
- 2 tbsp melted butter
- 1 tsp vanilla extract
- 1 apple, peeled, cored, and finely diced

Instructions:

1. In a large bowl, whisk together the flour, sugar, baking powder, baking soda, salt, and ground cinnamon.
2. In another bowl, whisk together the buttermilk, egg, melted butter, and vanilla extract until well combined.
3. Pour the wet ingredients into the dry ingredients and stir until just combined. Do not overmix; it's okay if the batter is a bit lumpy.
4. Gently fold in the diced apple into the batter.
5. Heat a non-stick skillet or griddle over medium heat and lightly grease with butter or cooking spray.
6. Pour 1/4 cup of batter onto the skillet for each pancake. Cook until bubbles form on the surface of the pancake and the edges look set, about 2-3 minutes.
7. Flip the pancakes and cook for another 1-2 minutes until golden brown and cooked through.
8. Serve warm with maple syrup, additional diced apples, and a sprinkle of cinnamon on top if desired.

Enjoy your delicious Cinnamon Apple Pancakes!

Cinnamon Sugar Pull-Apart Bread

Ingredients:

- 2 1/2 cups all-purpose flour
- 1/4 cup granulated sugar
- 2 1/4 tsp (1 packet) active dry yeast
- 1/2 tsp salt
- 1/2 cup milk, lukewarm
- 1/4 cup unsalted butter, melted
- 1 large egg
- 1 tsp vanilla extract

For the filling:

- 1/2 cup granulated sugar
- 2 tsp ground cinnamon
- 1/4 cup unsalted butter, melted

For the coating:

- 1/4 cup unsalted butter, melted
- 1/2 cup granulated sugar
- 1 tsp ground cinnamon

Instructions:

1. Prepare the dough:
    - In a large mixing bowl, combine 2 cups of flour, sugar, yeast, and salt.
    - In a separate bowl, whisk together the lukewarm milk, melted butter, egg, and vanilla extract.
    - Pour the wet ingredients into the dry ingredients and mix until a soft dough forms.
    - Gradually add the remaining 1/2 cup of flour as needed until the dough pulls away from the sides of the bowl.
    - Knead the dough on a lightly floured surface for about 5-7 minutes until smooth and elastic.
2. First rise:
    - Place the dough in a greased bowl, cover with a clean kitchen towel or plastic wrap, and let it rise in a warm place for about 1 hour or until doubled in size.
3. Prepare the filling:
    - In a small bowl, mix together the granulated sugar and ground cinnamon for the filling.
    - Melt the butter for the filling in another small bowl.
4. Assemble the bread:

- Punch down the risen dough and divide it into small pieces, about the size of golf balls.
- Roll each piece into a ball.
- Dip each ball into the melted butter for the filling, then roll in the cinnamon-sugar mixture until coated.

5. Layer in the pan:
   - Arrange the coated dough balls in a greased 9x5-inch loaf pan in layers, stacking them on top of each other.

6. Second rise:
   - Cover the loaf pan with a kitchen towel and let it rise again in a warm place for about 30-45 minutes, until puffy.

7. Bake:
   - Preheat the oven to 350°F (175°C).
   - Bake the bread for 30-35 minutes, or until golden brown and cooked through. If the top starts to brown too quickly, cover loosely with aluminum foil.

8. Finish:
   - Remove the bread from the oven and let it cool in the pan for about 10 minutes.
   - Carefully remove the bread from the pan and place it on a wire rack to cool slightly.

9. Coating:
   - While the bread is still warm, brush the top with melted butter and sprinkle with the cinnamon-sugar mixture.

10. Serve:
    - Pull apart the bread to serve, enjoying the layers of cinnamon-sugar goodness.

This Cinnamon Sugar Pull-Apart Bread is best served warm and is perfect for breakfast or as a sweet treat any time of day!

Cinnamon Rolls with Cream Cheese Frosting

Ingredients:

For the dough:

- 4 cups all-purpose flour
- 1/4 cup granulated sugar
- 1 tsp salt
- 2 1/4 tsp (1 packet) active dry yeast
- 3/4 cup milk, lukewarm
- 1/4 cup unsalted butter, melted
- 2 large eggs

For the filling:

- 1/2 cup unsalted butter, softened
- 1 cup packed brown sugar
- 2 tbsp ground cinnamon

For the cream cheese frosting:

- 4 oz cream cheese, softened
- 1/4 cup unsalted butter, softened
- 1 cup powdered sugar
- 1/2 tsp vanilla extract
- Pinch of salt

Instructions:

1. Prepare the dough:
    - In a large bowl, combine 3 cups of flour, sugar, salt, and yeast.
    - In a separate bowl, whisk together the lukewarm milk, melted butter, and eggs.
    - Pour the wet ingredients into the dry ingredients and mix until a dough forms.
    - Gradually add the remaining 1 cup of flour as needed until the dough is smooth and slightly sticky.
    - Knead the dough on a lightly floured surface for about 5-7 minutes until elastic.
    - Place the dough in a greased bowl, cover with a clean kitchen towel or plastic wrap, and let it rise in a warm place for about 1-1.5 hours until doubled in size.
2. Prepare the filling:
    - In a bowl, mix together the softened butter, brown sugar, and cinnamon until well combined.
3. Assemble the rolls:
    - Punch down the risen dough and roll it out on a lightly floured surface into a 16x12-inch rectangle.

- Spread the cinnamon filling evenly over the dough, leaving a small border around the edges.
4. Roll the dough:
    - Starting from one long edge, tightly roll up the dough into a log.
    - Pinch the seam to seal.
5. Cut the rolls:
    - Using a sharp knife or unflavored dental floss, cut the log into 12 even slices.
6. Second rise:
    - Place the rolls into a greased 9x13-inch baking pan.
    - Cover with a clean kitchen towel and let them rise in a warm place for about 30-45 minutes until puffy.
7. Bake:
    - Preheat the oven to 350°F (175°C).
    - Bake the rolls for 25-30 minutes until golden brown.
8. Make the cream cheese frosting:
    - In a bowl, beat together the softened cream cheese and butter until smooth.
    - Add powdered sugar, vanilla extract, and a pinch of salt. Beat until smooth and creamy.
9. Frost the rolls:
    - Spread the cream cheese frosting over the warm cinnamon rolls.
10. Serve:
    - Serve the cinnamon rolls warm. Enjoy the gooey, cinnamon-sugar goodness with the creamy frosting!

These homemade Cinnamon Rolls with Cream Cheese Frosting are sure to be a hit for breakfast or as a special treat any time of day.

Cinnamon Apple Pie

Ingredients:

For the crust:

- 2 1/2 cups all-purpose flour
- 1 tsp salt
- 1 cup unsalted butter, cold and cut into small cubes
- 6-8 tbsp ice water

For the filling:

- 6-7 medium-sized apples (such as Granny Smith or Honeycrisp), peeled, cored, and thinly sliced
- 3/4 cup granulated sugar
- 1/4 cup brown sugar
- 1 tbsp lemon juice
- 2 tbsp all-purpose flour
- 1 tsp ground cinnamon
- 1/4 tsp ground nutmeg
- 1/4 tsp salt

For assembling:

- 2 tbsp unsalted butter, cut into small pieces
- 1 egg, beaten (for egg wash)
- 1 tbsp granulated sugar mixed with 1/2 tsp ground cinnamon (for sprinkling)

Instructions:

1. Prepare the crust:
    - In a large bowl, whisk together the flour and salt.
    - Add the cold cubed butter to the flour mixture. Using a pastry cutter or your fingers, work the butter into the flour until the mixture resembles coarse crumbs.
    - Gradually add ice water, 1 tablespoon at a time, mixing with a fork until the dough just begins to hold together.
    - Divide the dough into two equal parts, shape each into a disk, wrap in plastic wrap, and refrigerate for at least 1 hour.
2. Preheat the oven:
    - Preheat your oven to 375°F (190°C).
3. Make the filling:
    - In a large bowl, combine the sliced apples, granulated sugar, brown sugar, lemon juice, flour, cinnamon, nutmeg, and salt. Toss until the apples are evenly coated.
4. Roll out the dough:

- On a lightly floured surface, roll out one disk of the chilled dough into a circle about 12 inches in diameter. Carefully transfer it to a 9-inch pie dish. Trim any excess dough hanging over the edges.
5. Assemble the pie:
    - Spoon the apple filling into the prepared pie crust, mounding it slightly in the center. Dot the filling with pieces of butter.
6. Roll out the top crust:
    - Roll out the second disk of chilled dough into a circle about 12 inches in diameter. Place it over the filling. Trim any excess dough, leaving about a 1-inch overhang.
7. Crimp the edges:
    - Fold the overhang of the top crust under the edge of the bottom crust. Crimp the edges using your fingers or a fork to seal the pie.
8. Ventilation:
    - Cut several slits in the top crust to allow steam to escape during baking.
9. Egg wash and sprinkle:
    - Brush the top crust with the beaten egg. Sprinkle the cinnamon-sugar mixture evenly over the top.
10. Bake:
    - Place the pie on a baking sheet (to catch any drips) and bake in the preheated oven for 45-55 minutes, or until the crust is golden brown and the filling is bubbling.
11. Cool and serve:
    - Allow the pie to cool on a wire rack for at least 2 hours before serving. This helps the filling set.
12. Serve:
    - Serve slices of Cinnamon Apple Pie warm or at room temperature, optionally with a scoop of vanilla ice cream or a dollop of whipped cream.

Enjoy the warm, comforting flavors of homemade Cinnamon Apple Pie with its buttery crust and perfectly spiced apple filling!

Cinnamon Swirl Coffee Cake

Ingredients:

For the cake:

- 2 cups all-purpose flour
- 1 tsp baking powder
- 1/2 tsp baking soda
- 1/2 tsp salt
- 1/2 cup unsalted butter, softened
- 1 cup granulated sugar
- 2 large eggs
- 1 tsp vanilla extract
- 1 cup sour cream or Greek yogurt

For the cinnamon swirl:

- 1/2 cup packed brown sugar
- 2 tsp ground cinnamon

For the streusel topping:

- 1/2 cup all-purpose flour
- 1/4 cup granulated sugar
- 1/4 cup packed brown sugar
- 1/2 tsp ground cinnamon
- 1/4 cup unsalted butter, melted

Instructions:

1. Preheat the oven:
    - Preheat your oven to 350°F (175°C). Grease and flour a 9x9-inch baking pan or line it with parchment paper for easy removal.
2. Make the cinnamon swirl:
    - In a small bowl, mix together the brown sugar and ground cinnamon for the swirl. Set aside.
3. Make the streusel topping:
    - In another bowl, combine the flour, granulated sugar, brown sugar, and cinnamon for the streusel.
    - Pour in the melted butter and mix until crumbly. Set aside.
4. Make the cake batter:
    - In a medium bowl, whisk together the flour, baking powder, baking soda, and salt.
    - In a large bowl, cream together the softened butter and granulated sugar until light and fluffy.

- Add the eggs one at a time, beating well after each addition.
- Stir in the vanilla extract.
- Gradually add the flour mixture to the butter mixture, alternating with the sour cream or Greek yogurt, beginning and ending with the flour mixture. Mix until just combined.

5. Assemble the coffee cake:
    - Spread half of the cake batter into the prepared baking pan, smoothing the top with a spatula.
    - Sprinkle the cinnamon swirl mixture evenly over the batter.
    - Carefully spread the remaining cake batter over the cinnamon swirl layer.
    - Sprinkle the streusel topping evenly over the top of the cake batter.
6. Bake:
    - Bake in the preheated oven for 40-45 minutes, or until a toothpick inserted into the center comes out clean or with just a few crumbs attached.
7. Cool and serve:
    - Allow the coffee cake to cool in the pan on a wire rack for at least 15-20 minutes before slicing and serving.
8. Optional glaze:
    - If desired, you can drizzle a simple powdered sugar glaze over the cooled coffee cake. Mix powdered sugar with a small amount of milk or water until you reach a drizzling consistency, then drizzle over the cake.

Enjoy your homemade Cinnamon Swirl Coffee Cake with a cup of coffee or tea for a delicious breakfast or snack!

Cinnamon Raisin Bread

Ingredients:

- 1 cup raisins
- 1/2 cup warm water
- 2 1/4 tsp (1 packet) active dry yeast
- 1/2 cup granulated sugar
- 1 cup warm milk (about 110°F or 45°C)
- 1/3 cup unsalted butter, melted
- 1 tsp salt
- 1 tsp ground cinnamon
- 4 1/2 - 5 cups all-purpose flour
- 1 egg, beaten (for egg wash)

For the cinnamon sugar filling:

- 1/4 cup granulated sugar
- 1 tbsp ground cinnamon

Instructions:

1. Activate the yeast:
    - In a small bowl, combine the warm water and yeast. Let it sit for 5-10 minutes until foamy.
2. Prepare the dough:
    - In a large bowl or the bowl of a stand mixer fitted with the dough hook attachment, combine the activated yeast mixture, granulated sugar, warm milk, melted butter, salt, and ground cinnamon.
    - Gradually add 4 cups of flour, one cup at a time, mixing until the dough comes together. The dough should be soft and slightly sticky. Add additional flour as needed, up to 1 cup more, to achieve the right consistency.
3. Knead the dough:
    - Turn the dough out onto a lightly floured surface and knead it for about 8-10 minutes, or knead it in the stand mixer for about 5-7 minutes, until smooth and elastic.
4. First rise:
    - Place the dough in a greased bowl, turning once to coat. Cover with a clean kitchen towel or plastic wrap and let it rise in a warm place for about 1-1.5 hours, or until doubled in size.
5. Prepare the filling:
    - In a small bowl, mix together the granulated sugar and ground cinnamon for the filling. Set aside.
6. Shape the bread:

- Punch down the risen dough to deflate it and turn it out onto a lightly floured surface.
- Roll the dough into a rectangle about 16x10 inches.

7. Add the filling:
    - Brush the dough with water (this helps the filling stick).
    - Sprinkle the cinnamon sugar mixture evenly over the dough.
    - Sprinkle the raisins evenly over the cinnamon sugar mixture.
8. Roll the dough:
    - Starting from one long edge, tightly roll up the dough into a log.
    - Pinch the seam to seal.
9. Second rise:
    - Place the rolled dough seam side down in a greased 9x5-inch loaf pan.
    - Cover with a clean kitchen towel and let it rise in a warm place for about 30-45 minutes, until puffy and nearly doubled in size.
10. Preheat the oven:
    - Preheat your oven to 350°F (175°C) during the last 15 minutes of the second rise.
11. Bake:
    - Brush the risen loaf gently with beaten egg to give it a shiny crust.
    - Bake in the preheated oven for 40-45 minutes, or until the bread is golden brown and sounds hollow when tapped on the bottom.
12. Cool and serve:
    - Remove the bread from the pan and transfer it to a wire rack to cool completely before slicing.

Enjoy slices of homemade Cinnamon Raisin Bread warm or toasted, with butter or cream cheese for a delightful treat!

Cinnamon French Toast

Ingredients:

- 4 slices of bread (thick slices like brioche or Texas toast work best)
- 2 large eggs
- 1/2 cup milk
- 1 tsp ground cinnamon
- 1/2 tsp vanilla extract
- 1 tbsp granulated sugar (optional, adjust to taste)
- Butter or cooking spray, for cooking
- Maple syrup, powdered sugar, or fresh berries, for serving

Instructions:

1. Prepare the egg mixture:
    - In a shallow bowl or pie plate, whisk together the eggs, milk, ground cinnamon, vanilla extract, and granulated sugar (if using) until well combined.
2. Dip the bread:
    - Heat a non-stick skillet or griddle over medium heat and add a pat of butter or coat with cooking spray.
    - Dip each slice of bread into the egg mixture, allowing it to soak for about 15-20 seconds on each side. Be sure the bread is evenly coated but not overly soaked to prevent it from becoming soggy.
3. Cook the French toast:
    - Place the dipped bread slices onto the preheated skillet or griddle. Cook for 2-3 minutes on each side, or until golden brown and cooked through. Adjust the heat as needed to prevent burning.
4. Serve:
    - Transfer the cooked French toast to a plate.
    - Serve warm with maple syrup, a dusting of powdered sugar, fresh berries, or any other toppings you prefer.

Tips for the best Cinnamon French Toast:

- Bread selection: Choose thick slices of bread like brioche, challah, or Texas toast. Sturdy breads hold up better to the soaking process.
- Egg mixture: Make sure the egg mixture is well whisked to evenly distribute the cinnamon and vanilla flavors throughout the French toast.
- Cooking temperature: Cooking over medium heat ensures that the French toast cooks evenly without burning. Adjust the heat as needed throughout the cooking process.
- Toppings: Customize your French toast with your favorite toppings such as fresh fruits, whipped cream, nuts, or a drizzle of chocolate sauce in addition to or instead of maple syrup.

Enjoy your homemade Cinnamon French Toast for a delightful breakfast or brunch!

Cinnamon Pecan Sticky Buns

Ingredients:

For the dough:

- 4 cups all-purpose flour
- 1/3 cup granulated sugar
- 1 tsp salt
- 2 1/4 tsp (1 packet) active dry yeast
- 1 cup milk, lukewarm
- 1/3 cup unsalted butter, melted
- 2 large eggs

For the filling:

- 1/2 cup unsalted butter, softened
- 1 cup packed brown sugar
- 2 tbsp ground cinnamon

For the sticky pecan topping:

- 1 cup chopped pecans
- 1/2 cup unsalted butter
- 1 cup packed brown sugar
- 1/4 cup heavy cream
- 1/4 cup honey or corn syrup

Instructions:

1. Make the dough:
    - In a large bowl, combine 3 cups of flour, granulated sugar, salt, and yeast.
    - In a separate bowl, whisk together the lukewarm milk, melted butter, and eggs.
    - Pour the wet ingredients into the dry ingredients and mix until a dough forms.
    - Gradually add the remaining 1 cup of flour as needed until the dough is smooth and slightly sticky.
    - Knead the dough on a lightly floured surface for about 5-7 minutes until elastic.
    - Place the dough in a greased bowl, cover with a clean kitchen towel or plastic wrap, and let it rise in a warm place for about 1 hour or until doubled in size.
2. Prepare the sticky pecan topping:
    - In a saucepan, melt 1/2 cup of butter over medium heat.
    - Stir in the brown sugar, heavy cream, and honey or corn syrup.
    - Bring the mixture to a boil, stirring constantly.
    - Remove from heat and stir in the chopped pecans.
    - Pour the sticky pecan mixture into the bottom of a greased 9x13-inch baking pan, spreading it evenly.

3. Make the filling:
   - In a small bowl, mix together the softened butter, brown sugar, and ground cinnamon until well combined. Set aside.
4. Assemble the sticky buns:
   - Punch down the risen dough and roll it out on a lightly floured surface into a rectangle about 16x12 inches.
   - Spread the cinnamon-sugar butter mixture evenly over the dough, leaving a small border around the edges.
5. Roll the dough:
   - Starting from one long edge, tightly roll up the dough into a log.
   - Pinch the seam to seal.
6. Cut the rolls:
   - Using a sharp knife or unflavored dental floss, cut the log into 12 even slices.
7. Second rise:
   - Place the rolls into the prepared baking pan on top of the sticky pecan topping.
   - Cover with a clean kitchen towel and let them rise in a warm place for about 30-45 minutes, until puffy.
8. Bake:
   - Preheat the oven to 350°F (175°C).
   - Bake the sticky buns for 30-35 minutes, or until golden brown and cooked through. If the tops start to brown too quickly, cover loosely with aluminum foil.
9. Cool and serve:
   - Allow the sticky buns to cool in the pan for about 5-10 minutes.
   - Place a serving platter or baking sheet over the pan and carefully invert to release the sticky buns onto the platter.
10. Enjoy:
    - Serve the warm and gooey Cinnamon Pecan Sticky Buns, allowing the caramelized pecan topping to drip down the sides.

These Cinnamon Pecan Sticky Buns are best enjoyed fresh and warm, perfect for a special breakfast or brunch treat!

Cinnamon Pear Crisp

Ingredients:

For the pear filling:

- 6-8 ripe pears, peeled, cored, and sliced (about 6 cups)
- 1/4 cup granulated sugar
- 1 tbsp lemon juice
- 1 tsp ground cinnamon
- 1/4 tsp ground nutmeg
- 1 tbsp cornstarch (optional, to thicken if needed)

For the crisp topping:

- 1 cup old-fashioned rolled oats
- 1/2 cup all-purpose flour
- 1/2 cup packed brown sugar
- 1/2 tsp ground cinnamon
- 1/4 tsp salt
- 1/2 cup unsalted butter, cold and cut into small pieces

Instructions:

1. Preheat the oven:
   - Preheat your oven to 350°F (175°C). Grease a 9x9-inch baking dish or a similar size baking dish.
2. Prepare the pear filling:
   - In a large bowl, toss the sliced pears with granulated sugar, lemon juice, ground cinnamon, and ground nutmeg.
   - If the pears are very juicy, sprinkle cornstarch over the mixture and toss to coat evenly. This helps to thicken the filling as it bakes.
3. Make the crisp topping:
   - In a separate bowl, combine the rolled oats, flour, brown sugar, ground cinnamon, and salt.
   - Cut in the cold butter pieces using a pastry cutter, fork, or your fingers until the mixture resembles coarse crumbs and the butter is well incorporated.
4. Assemble and bake:
   - Spread the prepared pear filling evenly into the greased baking dish.
   - Sprinkle the crisp topping evenly over the pear filling.
5. Bake the crisp:
   - Bake in the preheated oven for 40-45 minutes, or until the topping is golden brown and the pear filling is bubbly.
6. Cool and serve:

- Remove from the oven and let the Cinnamon Pear Crisp cool slightly before serving.
- Serve warm with a scoop of vanilla ice cream or a dollop of whipped cream, if desired.

Enjoy the warm, comforting flavors of Cinnamon Pear Crisp as a delightful dessert or even as a sweet treat for breakfast!

Cinnamon Almond Granola

Ingredients:

- 3 cups old-fashioned rolled oats
- 1 cup sliced almonds
- 1/2 cup unsweetened shredded coconut (optional)
- 1/2 cup pure maple syrup or honey
- 1/4 cup coconut oil or vegetable oil
- 1 tsp vanilla extract
- 1 tsp ground cinnamon
- 1/4 tsp salt
- 1 cup dried fruit of your choice (e.g., raisins, cranberries, chopped apricots) (optional)

Instructions:

1. Preheat the oven:
    - Preheat your oven to 300°F (150°C). Line a large baking sheet with parchment paper or a silicone baking mat.
2. Mix dry ingredients:
    - In a large bowl, combine the rolled oats, sliced almonds, and shredded coconut (if using). Mix well.
3. Prepare the wet ingredients:
    - In a small saucepan, heat the maple syrup or honey, coconut oil (or vegetable oil), vanilla extract, ground cinnamon, and salt over medium heat. Stir until the mixture is smooth and well combined. Remove from heat.
4. Combine wet and dry ingredients:
    - Pour the warm syrup mixture over the dry oat mixture. Stir until all the oats and nuts are evenly coated.
5. Bake the granola:
    - Spread the granola mixture evenly onto the prepared baking sheet.
    - Bake for 30-35 minutes, stirring halfway through, until the granola is golden brown and crisp. Keep an eye on it during the last few minutes to prevent burning.
6. Cool and add dried fruit (optional):
    - Remove the baking sheet from the oven and let the granola cool completely on the pan. It will crisp up as it cools.
    - Once cooled, stir in the dried fruit, if using.
7. Store the granola:
    - Transfer the cooled Cinnamon Almond Granola to an airtight container or mason jars for storage. It will keep well at room temperature for up to 2 weeks.
8. Serve:
    - Serve the granola as a snack on its own, with milk, yogurt, or sprinkle it over smoothie bowls and desserts.

Enjoy your homemade Cinnamon Almond Granola as a crunchy, flavorful addition to your breakfast or snack time! Adjust the sweetness and ingredients to suit your taste preferences.

Cinnamon Spice Cake

Ingredients:

For the cake:

- 2 cups all-purpose flour
- 1 1/2 tsp baking powder
- 1/2 tsp baking soda
- 1/2 tsp salt
- 2 tsp ground cinnamon
- 1/2 tsp ground nutmeg
- 1/4 tsp ground cloves
- 1/2 cup unsalted butter, softened
- 1 cup granulated sugar
- 1/2 cup brown sugar, packed
- 3 large eggs
- 1 tsp vanilla extract
- 1 cup buttermilk (or 1 cup milk mixed with 1 tbsp lemon juice or vinegar, let sit for 5 minutes)

For the cinnamon spice glaze:

- 1 cup powdered sugar
- 1/2 tsp ground cinnamon
- 2-3 tbsp milk or cream
- 1/2 tsp vanilla extract

Instructions:

1. Preheat oven and prepare pan:
   - Preheat your oven to 350°F (175°C). Grease and flour a 9-inch round cake pan or line it with parchment paper for easy removal.
2. Make the cake:
   - In a medium bowl, whisk together the flour, baking powder, baking soda, salt, cinnamon, nutmeg, and cloves until well combined.
3. Cream butter and sugars:
   - In a large bowl or the bowl of a stand mixer, cream together the softened butter, granulated sugar, and brown sugar until light and fluffy.
4. Add eggs and vanilla:
   - Beat in the eggs, one at a time, until well combined. Add the vanilla extract and mix until incorporated.
5. Alternate adding dry ingredients and buttermilk:

- Gradually add the dry ingredients to the butter mixture, alternating with the buttermilk, beginning and ending with the dry ingredients. Mix until just combined, being careful not to overmix.
6. Bake the cake:
    - Pour the batter into the prepared cake pan and spread it evenly with a spatula.
    - Bake in the preheated oven for 30-35 minutes, or until a toothpick inserted into the center comes out clean.
7. Cool the cake:
    - Remove the cake from the oven and let it cool in the pan for about 10 minutes. Then, transfer it to a wire rack to cool completely.
8. Make the cinnamon spice glaze:
    - In a small bowl, whisk together the powdered sugar, ground cinnamon, milk or cream, and vanilla extract until smooth and drizzle-able consistency. Adjust the milk or cream as needed to achieve your desired consistency.
9. Glaze the cake:
    - Once the cake has cooled completely, drizzle the cinnamon spice glaze over the top of the cake.
10. Serve:
    - Slice and serve the Cinnamon Spice Cake. Enjoy it with a hot beverage or as a delightful dessert!

This Cinnamon Spice Cake is sure to be a hit with its warm, comforting flavors and tender crumb. It's perfect for any occasion, from afternoon tea to special gatherings.

Cinnamon Banana Bread

Ingredients:

- 2-3 ripe bananas, mashed (about 1 cup)
- 1/3 cup unsalted butter, melted
- 3/4 cup granulated sugar
- 1 large egg, beaten
- 1 tsp vanilla extract
- 1 1/2 cups all-purpose flour
- 1 tsp baking powder
- 1/2 tsp baking soda
- 1/2 tsp salt
- 1 tsp ground cinnamon
- Optional: 1/2 cup chopped nuts (such as walnuts or pecans)

For the cinnamon sugar topping (optional):

- 1 tbsp granulated sugar
- 1/2 tsp ground cinnamon

Instructions:

1. Preheat oven and prepare pan:
    - Preheat your oven to 350°F (175°C). Grease a 9x5-inch loaf pan or line it with parchment paper.
2. Mash bananas:
    - In a medium bowl, mash the ripe bananas with a fork until smooth. You should have about 1 cup of mashed bananas.
3. Mix wet ingredients:
    - In a large bowl, combine the melted butter and granulated sugar. Stir until well combined.
    - Add the beaten egg and vanilla extract to the butter-sugar mixture. Mix until smooth.
4. Combine dry ingredients:
    - In a separate bowl, whisk together the flour, baking powder, baking soda, salt, and ground cinnamon.
5. Combine wet and dry ingredients:
    - Gradually add the dry ingredients to the wet ingredients, stirring until just combined. Be careful not to overmix. If using nuts, gently fold them into the batter.
6. Pour batter into pan:
    - Pour the batter into the prepared loaf pan, spreading it evenly with a spatula.
7. Optional cinnamon sugar topping:

- In a small bowl, mix together the granulated sugar and ground cinnamon for the topping.
- Sprinkle the cinnamon sugar mixture evenly over the top of the batter.
8. Bake:
    - Bake in the preheated oven for 60-70 minutes, or until a toothpick inserted into the center comes out clean or with a few moist crumbs attached.
9. Cool and serve:
    - Remove the banana bread from the oven and let it cool in the pan for about 10 minutes.
    - Then, transfer it to a wire rack to cool completely before slicing.
10. Enjoy:
    - Slice and serve the Cinnamon Banana Bread warm or at room temperature. It's delicious on its own or with a smear of butter.

This Cinnamon Banana Bread is moist, flavorful, and perfect for breakfast, brunch, or as a comforting snack any time of the day.

Cinnamon Pumpkin Muffins

Ingredients:

- 1 3/4 cups all-purpose flour
- 1 tsp baking soda
- 1/2 tsp baking powder
- 1/2 tsp salt
- 2 tsp ground cinnamon
- 1/2 tsp ground nutmeg
- 1/2 tsp ground ginger
- 1/4 tsp ground cloves
- 1 cup canned pumpkin puree
- 1/2 cup granulated sugar
- 1/2 cup brown sugar, packed
- 1/2 cup vegetable oil or melted butter
- 2 large eggs
- 1 tsp vanilla extract

For the cinnamon sugar topping:

- 1/4 cup granulated sugar
- 1 tsp ground cinnamon

Instructions:

1. Preheat oven and prepare muffin pan:
   - Preheat your oven to 375°F (190°C). Line a 12-cup muffin pan with paper liners or grease each cup lightly with cooking spray.
2. Mix dry ingredients:
   - In a medium bowl, whisk together the flour, baking soda, baking powder, salt, ground cinnamon, nutmeg, ginger, and cloves until well combined. Set aside.
3. Combine wet ingredients:
   - In a large bowl, whisk together the pumpkin puree, granulated sugar, brown sugar, vegetable oil or melted butter, eggs, and vanilla extract until smooth and well combined.
4. Combine wet and dry ingredients:
   - Gradually add the dry ingredients to the wet ingredients, stirring until just combined. Be careful not to overmix. The batter will be thick.
5. Fill muffin cups:
   - Divide the batter evenly among the prepared muffin cups, filling each about 2/3 full.
6. Make cinnamon sugar topping:
   - In a small bowl, mix together the granulated sugar and ground cinnamon for the topping.

7. Top muffins:
   - Sprinkle the cinnamon sugar mixture evenly over the tops of each muffin.
8. Bake:
   - Bake in the preheated oven for 18-20 minutes, or until a toothpick inserted into the center of a muffin comes out clean.
9. Cool and serve:
   - Remove the muffins from the oven and let them cool in the pan for 5 minutes.
   - Then, transfer them to a wire rack to cool completely.
10. Enjoy:
    - Serve these delicious Cinnamon Pumpkin Muffins warm or at room temperature. They are perfect for breakfast, brunch, or as a cozy snack!

These muffins are moist, flavorful, and full of autumn spices that will surely be a hit with family and friends. Adjust the sweetness or spices to suit your taste preferences for a perfect fall treat.

Cinnamon Apple Crumble Bars

Ingredients:

For the crust and crumble:

- 1 1/2 cups all-purpose flour
- 1 cup old-fashioned rolled oats
- 1/2 cup granulated sugar
- 1/2 cup packed brown sugar
- 1/2 tsp baking powder
- 1/4 tsp salt
- 1 tsp ground cinnamon
- 1 cup unsalted butter, cold and cut into small pieces

For the apple filling:

- 3 cups apples, peeled, cored, and diced (about 3-4 medium apples)
- 1 tbsp lemon juice
- 1/4 cup granulated sugar
- 1 tbsp all-purpose flour
- 1 tsp ground cinnamon
- 1/4 tsp ground nutmeg
- Pinch of salt

Instructions:

1. Preheat oven and prepare pan:
   - Preheat your oven to 350°F (175°C). Grease a 9x9-inch baking pan or line it with parchment paper for easy removal.
2. Make the crust and crumble:
   - In a large bowl, combine the flour, rolled oats, granulated sugar, brown sugar, baking powder, salt, and ground cinnamon.
   - Add the cold butter pieces and cut them into the dry ingredients using a pastry cutter or your fingers until the mixture resembles coarse crumbs. Set aside 1 1/2 cups of this mixture for the crumble topping.
3. Prepare the apple filling:
   - In another bowl, toss the diced apples with lemon juice.
   - Add granulated sugar, flour, ground cinnamon, ground nutmeg, and a pinch of salt to the apples. Toss until the apples are evenly coated.
4. Assemble the bars:
   - Press the remaining crumb mixture firmly into the bottom of the prepared baking pan to form the crust.
   - Spread the apple filling evenly over the crust.
5. Add the crumble topping:

- Sprinkle the reserved crumble mixture evenly over the apple filling, covering it completely.
6. Bake:
    - Bake in the preheated oven for 45-50 minutes, or until the top is golden brown and the apple filling is bubbling around the edges.
7. Cool and slice:
    - Remove the pan from the oven and let it cool completely on a wire rack.
    - Once cooled, lift the bars out of the pan using the parchment paper and transfer them to a cutting board.
    - Slice into squares or rectangles.
8. Serve:
    - Serve these delicious Cinnamon Apple Crumble Bars as a delightful dessert or snack. They are delicious warm or at room temperature.

These bars are perfect for fall, combining the flavors of cinnamon-spiced apples with a buttery crumble topping. Enjoy them with a scoop of vanilla ice cream or a drizzle of caramel sauce for an extra treat!

Cinnamon Ginger Cookies

Ingredients:

- 2 1/4 cups all-purpose flour
- 2 tsp ground ginger
- 1 tsp ground cinnamon
- 1/2 tsp ground cloves
- 1/2 tsp ground nutmeg
- 1/2 tsp baking soda
- 1/4 tsp salt
- 3/4 cup unsalted butter, softened
- 1 cup granulated sugar
- 1/4 cup molasses
- 1 large egg
- 1/2 cup granulated sugar (for rolling)

Instructions:

1. Preheat oven:
    - Preheat your oven to 350°F (175°C). Line baking sheets with parchment paper or silicone mats.
2. Mix dry ingredients:
    - In a medium bowl, whisk together the flour, ground ginger, ground cinnamon, ground cloves, ground nutmeg, baking soda, and salt. Set aside.
3. Cream butter and sugar:
    - In a large bowl or the bowl of a stand mixer fitted with the paddle attachment, cream together the softened butter and 1 cup of granulated sugar until light and fluffy, about 2-3 minutes.
4. Add molasses and egg:
    - Add the molasses and egg to the butter-sugar mixture. Beat until well combined.
5. Combine wet and dry ingredients:
    - Gradually add the dry ingredients to the wet ingredients, mixing on low speed until just combined. Scrape down the sides of the bowl as needed to ensure even mixing.
6. Chill the dough (optional):
    - For easier handling, you can chill the dough in the refrigerator for about 30 minutes to 1 hour. Chilling will also help the flavors meld together.
7. Roll dough into balls:
    - Place the remaining 1/2 cup of granulated sugar in a small bowl.
    - Roll the dough into 1-inch balls, then roll each ball in the granulated sugar until coated.
8. Place on baking sheets:
    - Arrange the cookie dough balls on the prepared baking sheets, spacing them about 2 inches apart to allow for spreading during baking.

9. Bake:
    - Bake in the preheated oven for 10-12 minutes, or until the edges are set and the tops of the cookies are cracked.
10. Cool and serve:
    - Remove the cookies from the oven and let them cool on the baking sheets for 5 minutes.
    - Then, transfer the cookies to a wire rack to cool completely.
11. Enjoy:
    - Serve these Cinnamon Ginger Cookies with a glass of milk, hot cocoa, or your favorite warm beverage. They also make a wonderful homemade gift or holiday treat!

These cookies are soft, chewy, and full of delicious spice flavors. They're perfect for any occasion and are sure to be a hit with family and friends!

Cinnamon Honey Butter

Ingredients:

- 1/2 cup (1 stick) unsalted butter, softened
- 2 tbsp honey
- 1/2 tsp ground cinnamon
- Pinch of salt (optional)

Instructions:

1. Prepare the butter:
   - In a small mixing bowl, add the softened butter.
2. Add honey and cinnamon:
   - Pour in the honey and sprinkle the ground cinnamon over the butter.
3. Mix thoroughly:
   - Using a spoon or a hand mixer, blend the ingredients together until smooth and well combined. Ensure that the honey and cinnamon are evenly distributed throughout the butter.
4. Adjust consistency (optional):
   - If the butter is too soft, you can chill it in the refrigerator for a short while to firm up. Alternatively, if you prefer a softer spread, you can leave it at room temperature.
5. Serve or store:
   - Transfer the Cinnamon Honey Butter to a small serving bowl or airtight container.
   - Serve immediately as a spread for toast, muffins, pancakes, waffles, or biscuits. It also pairs well with fresh fruit.
   - If not serving right away, store the butter in the refrigerator. Before serving again, allow it to soften slightly at room temperature for easier spreading.

Tips:

- Variations: You can adjust the amount of honey or cinnamon based on your taste preferences. Some people prefer a stronger cinnamon flavor, while others may prefer a more subtle sweetness.
- Uses: Besides using it as a spread, Cinnamon Honey Butter can be melted and drizzled over pancakes or used to glaze baked goods.

This homemade Cinnamon Honey Butter adds a delicious twist to your breakfast or snack, providing a delightful combination of flavors that everyone will enjoy.

Cinnamon Peach Cobbler

Ingredients:

For the peach filling:

- 6 cups fresh or canned peach slices (about 6-8 peaches, peeled and sliced)
- 1/2 cup granulated sugar (adjust based on sweetness of peaches)
- 1/4 cup brown sugar
- 1 tbsp lemon juice
- 1 tsp vanilla extract
- 1/2 tsp ground cinnamon
- 2 tbsp cornstarch

For the biscuit topping:

- 1 cup all-purpose flour
- 1/4 cup granulated sugar
- 1 tsp baking powder
- 1/4 tsp baking soda
- 1/4 tsp salt
- 1/2 tsp ground cinnamon
- 6 tbsp cold unsalted butter, cut into small pieces
- 1/3 cup buttermilk (or regular milk)

For sprinkling on top:

- 1 tbsp granulated sugar mixed with 1/2 tsp ground cinnamon

Instructions:

1. Preheat oven:
    - Preheat your oven to 375°F (190°C). Butter a 9x13-inch baking dish or a similar size casserole dish.
2. Prepare the peach filling:
    - In a large bowl, combine the peach slices, granulated sugar, brown sugar, lemon juice, vanilla extract, ground cinnamon, and cornstarch. Stir gently to coat the peaches evenly. Set aside while you prepare the topping.
3. Make the biscuit topping:
    - In a separate bowl, whisk together the flour, granulated sugar, baking powder, baking soda, salt, and ground cinnamon.
    - Cut in the cold butter pieces using a pastry cutter or your fingers until the mixture resembles coarse crumbs.
    - Stir in the buttermilk (or regular milk) until just combined. The dough should be slightly sticky.
4. Assemble the cobbler:

- Spread the peach filling evenly into the prepared baking dish.
5. Add the biscuit topping:
    - Drop spoonfuls of the biscuit topping evenly over the peaches. It's okay if some of the peaches are peeking through.
6. Sprinkle with cinnamon sugar:
    - Mix together 1 tablespoon of granulated sugar with 1/2 teaspoon of ground cinnamon. Sprinkle this mixture evenly over the top of the biscuit topping.
7. Bake the cobbler:
    - Place the baking dish in the preheated oven and bake for 35-40 minutes, or until the topping is golden brown and the peach filling is bubbling around the edges.
8. Cool slightly and serve:
    - Remove the cobbler from the oven and let it cool for 10-15 minutes before serving.
    - Serve warm with a scoop of vanilla ice cream or a dollop of whipped cream, if desired.
9. Enjoy:
    - Enjoy this delicious Cinnamon Peach Cobbler as a comforting dessert, perfect for any occasion, especially during peach season!

This Cinnamon Peach Cobbler recipe captures the essence of summer with its juicy peach filling and spiced biscuit topping, making it a favorite for family gatherings and casual dinners alike.

Cinnamon Oatmeal Raisin Cookies

Ingredients:

- 1 cup unsalted butter, softened
- 1 cup packed light brown sugar
- 1/2 cup granulated sugar
- 2 large eggs
- 1 tsp vanilla extract
- 1 1/2 cups all-purpose flour
- 1 tsp ground cinnamon
- 1/2 tsp baking soda
- 1/2 tsp salt
- 3 cups old-fashioned rolled oats
- 1 cup raisins (you can also use a mix of raisins and chopped nuts if desired)

Instructions:

1. Preheat oven:
    - Preheat your oven to 350°F (175°C). Line baking sheets with parchment paper or silicone baking mats.
2. Cream butter and sugars:
    - In a large bowl or the bowl of a stand mixer, cream together the softened butter, brown sugar, and granulated sugar until light and fluffy.
3. Add eggs and vanilla:
    - Add the eggs, one at a time, beating well after each addition. Mix in the vanilla extract until well combined.
4. Combine dry ingredients:
    - In a separate bowl, whisk together the flour, ground cinnamon, baking soda, and salt.
5. Combine wet and dry ingredients:
    - Gradually add the dry ingredients to the butter-sugar mixture, mixing on low speed until just combined.
6. Add oats and raisins:
    - Stir in the rolled oats and raisins (or raisins and nuts) until evenly distributed throughout the dough.
7. Chill the dough (optional):
    - For thicker cookies, you can chill the dough in the refrigerator for about 30 minutes to 1 hour.
8. Form cookie dough balls:
    - Scoop dough by rounded tablespoons and place them onto the prepared baking sheets, spacing them about 2 inches apart.
9. Bake:
    - Bake in the preheated oven for 10-12 minutes, or until the edges are lightly golden brown.

10. Cool and serve:
    - Remove from the oven and let the cookies cool on the baking sheets for a few minutes before transferring them to wire racks to cool completely.
11. Enjoy:
    - Enjoy these delicious Cinnamon Oatmeal Raisin Cookies with a glass of milk, hot cocoa, or your favorite warm beverage. They're perfect for snacking or as a homemade treat!

These cookies are chewy, flavorful, and perfect for any time of day. The combination of cinnamon, oats, and plump raisins makes them a favorite among cookie lovers of all ages.

Cinnamon Chocolate Chip Scones

Ingredients:

- 2 cups all-purpose flour
- 1/3 cup granulated sugar
- 1 tbsp baking powder
- 1/2 tsp salt
- 1 tsp ground cinnamon
- 1/2 cup cold unsalted butter, cut into small pieces
- 1/2 cup chocolate chips (semi-sweet or milk chocolate)
- 1/2 cup milk (plus extra for brushing)
- 1 large egg
- 1 tsp vanilla extract

For the cinnamon sugar topping:

- 1 tbsp granulated sugar
- 1/2 tsp ground cinnamon

Instructions:

1. Preheat oven and prepare baking sheet:
    - Preheat your oven to 400°F (200°C). Line a baking sheet with parchment paper or a silicone baking mat.
2. Mix dry ingredients:
    - In a large bowl, whisk together the flour, granulated sugar, baking powder, salt, and ground cinnamon.
3. Cut in butter:
    - Add the cold butter pieces to the flour mixture. Using a pastry cutter or your fingers, cut the butter into the flour until the mixture resembles coarse crumbs and the butter is pea-sized.
4. Add chocolate chips:
    - Stir in the chocolate chips until evenly distributed throughout the flour mixture.
5. Mix wet ingredients:
    - In a separate bowl, whisk together the milk, egg, and vanilla extract until well combined.
6. Combine wet and dry ingredients:
    - Pour the wet ingredients into the dry ingredients. Stir gently with a fork or spatula until the dough starts to come together. It will be slightly crumbly.
7. Form the dough:
    - Turn the dough out onto a lightly floured surface. Gently knead the dough a few times until it holds together. Do not overwork the dough.
8. Shape and cut scones:

- Pat the dough into a circle about 1 inch thick. Use a sharp knife or a bench scraper to cut the circle into 8 wedges.
9. Prepare cinnamon sugar topping:
    - In a small bowl, mix together the granulated sugar and ground cinnamon for the topping.
10. Brush with milk and sprinkle topping:
    - Place the scones on the prepared baking sheet. Brush the tops with a little milk and sprinkle evenly with the cinnamon sugar topping.
11. Bake:
    - Bake in the preheated oven for 15-18 minutes, or until the scones are golden brown and cooked through.
12. Cool and serve:
    - Remove from the oven and let the scones cool on the baking sheet for a few minutes before transferring them to a wire rack to cool completely.
13. Enjoy:
    - Serve these delicious Cinnamon Chocolate Chip Scones warm or at room temperature with a cup of tea or coffee. They are perfect for breakfast or as a tasty snack!

These scones are buttery, tender, and bursting with the flavors of cinnamon and chocolate chips. They are sure to be a hit with family and friends!

Cinnamon Maple Glazed Carrots

Ingredients:

- 1 lb (about 450g) carrots, peeled and sliced into 1/4-inch thick rounds or diagonally
- 2 tbsp unsalted butter
- 1/4 cup maple syrup
- 1/2 tsp ground cinnamon
- Salt and pepper, to taste
- Chopped fresh parsley or cilantro, for garnish (optional)

Instructions:

1. Prepare the carrots:
    - Peel the carrots and slice them into 1/4-inch thick rounds or diagonally for a more elegant presentation.
2. Cook the carrots:
    - In a large skillet or frying pan, melt the butter over medium heat. Add the sliced carrots to the skillet.
3. Saute the carrots:
    - Cook the carrots, stirring occasionally, for about 5-7 minutes or until they begin to soften slightly.
4. Add maple syrup and cinnamon:
    - Pour the maple syrup over the carrots in the skillet. Sprinkle ground cinnamon evenly over the carrots.
5. Simmer and glaze:
    - Stir the carrots gently to coat them evenly with the maple syrup and cinnamon mixture. Reduce the heat to medium-low.
6. Cover and cook:
    - Cover the skillet with a lid and let the carrots simmer for another 5-8 minutes, or until they are tender and glazed, stirring occasionally.
7. Season to taste:
    - Once the carrots are cooked to your desired tenderness and glazed with the syrup mixture, season with salt and pepper to taste. Adjust the sweetness or spiciness by adding more cinnamon or maple syrup if desired.
8. Serve:
    - Transfer the glazed carrots to a serving dish. Garnish with chopped fresh parsley or cilantro if desired for a pop of color and freshness.
9. Enjoy:
    - Serve these Cinnamon Maple Glazed Carrots warm as a delicious side dish alongside roasted meats, poultry, or as part of a festive holiday meal.

These glazed carrots are sure to impress with their sweet and savory flavors, making them a perfect addition to your dinner table any time of year. Adjust the seasoning and sweetness to suit your taste preferences for a delightful culinary experience.

Cinnamon Cranberry Sauce

Ingredients:

- 12 ounces (about 3 cups) fresh cranberries
- 1 cup granulated sugar
- 1/2 cup water
- 1 cinnamon stick
- 1/2 tsp ground cinnamon
- Zest of 1 orange (optional)
- Juice of 1 orange (about 1/4 cup, optional)

Instructions:

1. Prepare the cranberries:
    - Rinse the fresh cranberries under cold water and discard any damaged berries or debris.
2. Combine ingredients in a saucepan:
    - In a medium saucepan, combine the cranberries, granulated sugar, water, cinnamon stick, and ground cinnamon.
    - If using, add the orange zest and juice for extra flavor.
3. Cook over medium heat:
    - Bring the mixture to a boil over medium heat, stirring occasionally.
4. Simmer:
    - Reduce the heat to low and let the cranberry sauce simmer for about 10-15 minutes, or until the cranberries burst and the sauce thickens to your desired consistency. Stir occasionally to prevent sticking.
5. Mash or leave whole (optional):
    - For a smoother sauce, use a potato masher or the back of a spoon to gently mash some of the cranberries during cooking.
    - For a chunkier sauce, leave the cranberries whole.
6. Remove cinnamon stick:
    - Once the sauce has thickened and the cranberries are cooked, remove the cinnamon stick from the saucepan.
7. Cool and serve:
    - Let the Cinnamon Cranberry Sauce cool to room temperature.
    - Transfer the sauce to a serving bowl or storage container. It will continue to thicken as it cools.
8. Chill (optional):
    - If you prefer chilled cranberry sauce, refrigerate it for at least 2 hours before serving. It can be stored in the refrigerator for up to 1 week.
9. Enjoy:
    - Serve this homemade Cinnamon Cranberry Sauce as a delicious accompaniment to roast turkey, chicken, pork, or even as a spread on sandwiches or toast. It adds a festive touch to any holiday meal!

This Cinnamon Cranberry Sauce is bursting with flavor and can be adjusted to your taste preferences by adding more or less sugar, cinnamon, or orange zest. It's a versatile condiment that enhances both savory and sweet dishes during the holiday season and beyond.

Cinnamon Vanilla Rice Pudding

Ingredients:

- 1 cup long-grain white rice
- 4 cups whole milk
- 1/2 cup granulated sugar
- 1/4 tsp salt
- 1 cinnamon stick
- 1 tsp vanilla extract
- Ground cinnamon, for sprinkling (optional)
- Fresh berries or fruit, for serving (optional)

Instructions:

1. Rinse and prepare the rice:
    - Rinse the rice under cold water until the water runs clear. This helps remove excess starch.
2. Cook the rice:
    - In a large saucepan, combine the rinsed rice, whole milk, granulated sugar, salt, and cinnamon stick.
    - Bring the mixture to a boil over medium-high heat, stirring occasionally to prevent the rice from sticking to the bottom of the pan.
3. Simmer:
    - Once the mixture reaches a boil, reduce the heat to low. Cover the saucepan with a lid, leaving it slightly ajar to allow steam to escape.
    - Let the rice simmer gently for about 25-30 minutes, stirring occasionally, until the rice is tender and the mixture has thickened to a creamy consistency.
4. Add vanilla extract:
    - Remove the saucepan from the heat. Discard the cinnamon stick.
    - Stir in the vanilla extract until well combined.
5. Serve:
    - Spoon the Cinnamon Vanilla Rice Pudding into individual serving bowls or glasses.
    - Optionally, sprinkle ground cinnamon on top for added flavor and decoration.
6. Chill (optional):
    - If you prefer chilled rice pudding, let it cool to room temperature and then refrigerate for at least 1-2 hours before serving.
7. Garnish and enjoy:
    - Serve the Cinnamon Vanilla Rice Pudding warm or chilled.
    - Optionally, garnish with fresh berries or fruit for a refreshing contrast.
8. Storage:
    - Store any leftover rice pudding in an airtight container in the refrigerator for up to 3 days. Reheat gently before serving if desired.

This Cinnamon Vanilla Rice Pudding is a comforting dessert that can be enjoyed warm or chilled, making it perfect for any occasion. The combination of cinnamon and vanilla creates a delightful aroma and flavor that is sure to please your taste buds.

Cinnamon Sweet Potato Casserole

Ingredients:

For the sweet potato base:

- 4 cups mashed sweet potatoes (about 3-4 large sweet potatoes)
- 1/2 cup granulated sugar
- 1/4 cup unsalted butter, melted
- 1/2 cup milk (whole milk or evaporated milk)
- 2 large eggs
- 1 tsp vanilla extract
- 1/2 tsp ground cinnamon
- 1/4 tsp ground nutmeg
- 1/4 tsp salt

For the pecan streusel topping:

- 1/2 cup all-purpose flour
- 1/2 cup packed brown sugar
- 1/4 cup unsalted butter, melted
- 1/2 cup chopped pecans
- 1/2 tsp ground cinnamon

Instructions:

1. Preheat oven and prepare baking dish:
    - Preheat your oven to 350°F (175°C). Grease a 9x13-inch baking dish with butter or cooking spray.
2. Cook and mash sweet potatoes:
    - Peel and cut the sweet potatoes into chunks. Place them in a large pot of water and bring to a boil. Cook until fork-tender, about 15-20 minutes. Drain and mash the sweet potatoes until smooth.
3. Prepare the sweet potato base:
    - In a large mixing bowl, combine the mashed sweet potatoes, granulated sugar, melted butter, milk, eggs, vanilla extract, ground cinnamon, ground nutmeg, and salt. Mix until well combined and smooth.
4. Transfer to baking dish:
    - Spread the sweet potato mixture evenly into the prepared baking dish, smoothing the top with a spatula.
5. Make the pecan streusel topping:
    - In a separate bowl, combine the flour, brown sugar, melted butter, chopped pecans, and ground cinnamon. Mix with a fork until crumbly.
6. Top the casserole:

- Sprinkle the pecan streusel topping evenly over the sweet potato mixture in the baking dish, covering it completely.
7. Bake:
    - Bake in the preheated oven for 30-35 minutes, or until the topping is golden brown and the sweet potato mixture is heated through.
8. Cool and serve:
    - Remove from the oven and let the casserole cool for 10-15 minutes before serving.
9. Enjoy:
    - Serve this delicious Cinnamon Sweet Potato Casserole as a side dish for holiday dinners or any special occasion. It pairs well with roasted meats, poultry, or as part of a vegetarian meal.

This casserole is sure to become a favorite with its creamy sweet potato base and crunchy, cinnamon-spiced pecan streusel topping. It's a comforting and festive dish that will delight your family and guests alike!

Cinnamon Hazelnut Latte

Ingredients:

- 1 shot of espresso (or 1/2 cup strong brewed coffee)
- 1 cup milk (any type you prefer: whole milk, 2%, almond milk, etc.)
- 1 tbsp hazelnut syrup (adjust to taste)
- 1/4 tsp ground cinnamon
- Whipped cream (optional, for topping)
- Ground cinnamon or cocoa powder, for garnish (optional)

Instructions:

1. Brew the espresso:
    - Brew one shot of espresso using an espresso machine. Alternatively, you can brew strong coffee using a French press or drip coffee maker.
2. Heat the milk:
    - In a small saucepan or using a milk frother, heat the milk until it is steaming hot. Froth the milk if desired to create a creamy texture.
3. Prepare the latte:
    - Pour the hot espresso into a large mug.
    - Stir in the hazelnut syrup and ground cinnamon until well combined.
4. Add the steamed milk:
    - Pour the steamed milk into the mug with the espresso mixture, holding back the foam with a spoon if you prefer more milk than foam.
5. Top with foam (optional):
    - Spoon any remaining foam on top of the latte.
6. Garnish and serve:
    - If desired, top with whipped cream and sprinkle with a pinch of ground cinnamon or cocoa powder for extra flavor and presentation.
7. Enjoy:
    - Serve your homemade Cinnamon Hazelnut Latte immediately while it's warm and cozy.

This latte is perfect for enjoying on a chilly morning or as an afternoon pick-me-up. Adjust the sweetness by adding more or less hazelnut syrup to suit your taste preferences. It's a delicious treat that brings together the comforting flavors of cinnamon and hazelnut with the richness of espresso.

Cinnamon Cherry Jam

Ingredients:

- 4 cups pitted and chopped cherries (about 2 lbs of cherries)
- 2 cups granulated sugar
- Juice of 1 lemon (about 2-3 tbsp)
- 1 cinnamon stick
- 1/2 tsp ground cinnamon
- Pinch of salt

Instructions:

1. Prepare the cherries:
    - Wash the cherries thoroughly. Remove the pits and chop them into small pieces. Measure out 4 cups of chopped cherries.
2. Cook the cherries:
    - In a large, heavy-bottomed saucepan, combine the chopped cherries, granulated sugar, lemon juice, cinnamon stick, ground cinnamon, and a pinch of salt.
3. Bring to a boil:
    - Stir the mixture over medium-high heat until the sugar dissolves completely. Bring the mixture to a boil, stirring frequently to prevent sticking.
4. Simmer:
    - Reduce the heat to medium-low and let the mixture simmer gently. Stir occasionally to prevent burning, and skim off any foam that forms on the surface.
5. Cook until thickened:
    - Cook the jam for about 30-40 minutes, or until it thickens to your desired consistency. To test if the jam is ready, place a small amount on a chilled plate and tilt it. If it holds its shape without being too runny, it's done.
6. Remove cinnamon stick:
    - Once the jam has thickened, remove the cinnamon stick from the saucepan.
7. Cool and store:
    - Let the Cinnamon Cherry Jam cool slightly before transferring it into clean, sterilized jars. Seal the jars tightly.
8. Optional canning (for long-term storage):
    - If you plan to store the jam for an extended period, you can process the jars in a boiling water bath for 10 minutes to seal them properly.
9. Enjoy:
    - Enjoy your homemade Cinnamon Cherry Jam on toast, biscuits, yogurt, or use it as a topping for desserts. It also makes a lovely gift!

This Cinnamon Cherry Jam recipe captures the essence of fresh cherries with a touch of cinnamon, creating a flavorful spread that is perfect for breakfast or as an accompaniment to various dishes. Adjust the sweetness or cinnamon flavor according to your taste preferences for a personalized jam experience.

Cinnamon Coconut Macaroons

Ingredients:

- 3 cups shredded coconut (sweetened or unsweetened)
- 3/4 cup sweetened condensed milk
- 1 tsp vanilla extract
- 1/2 tsp ground cinnamon
- 1/4 tsp salt
- 2 large egg whites
- 1/4 cup granulated sugar

Instructions:

1. Preheat oven:
    - Preheat your oven to 325°F (160°C). Line a baking sheet with parchment paper or a silicone baking mat.
2. Mix coconut mixture:
    - In a large bowl, combine the shredded coconut, sweetened condensed milk, vanilla extract, ground cinnamon, and salt. Stir until well combined.
3. Whip egg whites:
    - In a separate bowl, use an electric mixer or a whisk to beat the egg whites until soft peaks form. Gradually add the granulated sugar while continuing to beat until stiff peaks form.
4. Fold in egg whites:
    - Gently fold the whipped egg whites into the coconut mixture until fully incorporated. Be careful not to deflate the egg whites too much.
5. Form macaroons:
    - Scoop tablespoon-sized mounds of the coconut mixture onto the prepared baking sheet, spacing them about 1 inch apart.
6. Bake:
    - Bake in the preheated oven for 20-25 minutes, or until the edges of the macaroons are golden brown and the tops are lightly golden.
7. Cool:
    - Remove the macaroons from the oven and let them cool on the baking sheet for a few minutes. Then, transfer them to a wire rack to cool completely.
8. Enjoy:
    - Once cooled, these Cinnamon Coconut Macaroons are ready to enjoy! They can be stored in an airtight container at room temperature for several days.

These macaroons are chewy on the inside with a slightly crisp exterior, and the combination of coconut and cinnamon adds a delightful twist to the classic recipe. They make a perfect treat for parties, gatherings, or simply as a sweet snack with a cup of tea or coffee.

Cinnamon Lemonade

Ingredients:

- 1 cup freshly squeezed lemon juice (about 4-6 lemons)
- 4 cups cold water
- 1/2 cup granulated sugar (adjust to taste)
- 2 cinnamon sticks
- Ice cubes
- Lemon slices and cinnamon sticks, for garnish (optional)

Instructions:

1. Make simple syrup:
   - In a small saucepan, combine 1 cup of water with the granulated sugar and cinnamon sticks. Bring to a boil over medium-high heat, stirring until the sugar is dissolved. Let it simmer for 1-2 minutes. Remove from heat and let the cinnamon sticks steep in the syrup as it cools.
2. Prepare lemon juice:
   - While the syrup cools, juice the lemons to get 1 cup of fresh lemon juice.
3. Combine lemon juice and water:
   - In a large pitcher, combine the freshly squeezed lemon juice with 3 cups of cold water.
4. Add cinnamon syrup:
   - Once the cinnamon syrup has cooled to room temperature, strain out the cinnamon sticks and pour the syrup into the pitcher with the lemon juice and water mixture. Stir well to combine.
5. Chill:
   - Refrigerate the Cinnamon Lemonade for at least 1 hour to chill and allow the flavors to meld together.
6. Serve:
   - Fill glasses with ice cubes and pour the chilled Cinnamon Lemonade over the ice.
7. Garnish (optional):
   - Garnish each glass with a slice of lemon and a cinnamon stick for presentation.
8. Enjoy:
   - Stir before serving and enjoy this refreshing Cinnamon Lemonade on a hot day or as a unique twist for any occasion!

This Cinnamon Lemonade is not only refreshing but also has a warm, comforting undertone from the cinnamon syrup, making it a delightful drink to enjoy during warm weather or as a special treat any time of year. Adjust the sweetness and cinnamon flavor to suit your taste preferences for a perfectly balanced beverage.

Cinnamon Apricot Chutney

Ingredients:

- 1 lb (about 450g) fresh apricots, pitted and chopped
- 1 cup granulated sugar
- 1/2 cup apple cider vinegar
- 1 small onion, finely chopped
- 1/2 cup raisins or currants
- 1/2 tsp ground cinnamon
- 1/4 tsp ground cloves
- 1/4 tsp ground ginger
- 1/4 tsp salt
- 1/4 tsp black pepper

Instructions:

1. Prepare the apricots:
    - Rinse the apricots, remove the pits, and chop them into small pieces. You can leave the skins on.
2. Cook the chutney:
    - In a large saucepan, combine the chopped apricots, granulated sugar, apple cider vinegar, finely chopped onion, raisins or currants, ground cinnamon, ground cloves, ground ginger, salt, and black pepper.
3. Simmer:
    - Bring the mixture to a boil over medium-high heat, stirring frequently to dissolve the sugar.
4. Reduce heat:
    - Reduce the heat to low and let the chutney simmer gently, uncovered, for about 30-40 minutes. Stir occasionally to prevent sticking.
5. Cook until thickened:
    - Cook the chutney until it thickens to a jam-like consistency and the apricots are soft and cooked down.
6. Adjust seasoning:
    - Taste the chutney and adjust the seasoning if needed. You can add more sugar for sweetness or more vinegar for acidity, according to your preference.
7. Cool and store:
    - Remove the cinnamon apricot chutney from the heat and let it cool to room temperature.
8. Serve or store:
    - Transfer the cooled chutney to clean, sterilized jars or containers. Seal tightly and refrigerate for up to 2 weeks. For longer storage, you can process the jars in a water bath for 10 minutes to seal them properly.
9. Enjoy:

- Serve this delicious Cinnamon Apricot Chutney as a condiment with cheese platters, grilled meats, sandwiches, or as a flavorful addition to your favorite dishes!

This chutney has a wonderful balance of sweet and savory flavors, with the warmth of cinnamon adding a delightful twist to the sweetness of apricots. It's perfect for adding a burst of flavor to your meals or as a homemade gift for friends and family.

Cinnamon Whipped Cream

Ingredients:

- 1 cup cold heavy cream
- 2 tbsp powdered sugar (adjust to taste)
- 1/2 tsp ground cinnamon
- 1/2 tsp vanilla extract (optional)

Instructions:

1. Chill equipment:
    - Place a mixing bowl and beaters or whisk attachment in the refrigerator for about 15-20 minutes before you start. This helps keep the cream cold and makes it whip faster.
2. Whip the cream:
    - Remove the chilled bowl and beaters from the refrigerator. Pour the cold heavy cream into the bowl.
3. Add sugar and cinnamon:
    - Sprinkle the powdered sugar and ground cinnamon over the cream.
4. Start whipping:
    - Using a hand mixer or stand mixer fitted with the whisk attachment, start whipping the cream on low speed to incorporate the sugar and cinnamon.
5. Increase speed:
    - Gradually increase the speed to medium-high and continue whipping until soft peaks form. This means the cream will hold its shape but still have a slight curl at the peak when you lift the beaters.
6. Add vanilla extract (optional):
    - If using vanilla extract, add it during the whipping process and continue beating until combined.
7. Check consistency:
    - Be careful not to over-whip the cream, as it can quickly turn into butter. Stop whipping when you reach the desired consistency.
8. Serve or store:
    - Use the cinnamon whipped cream immediately as a topping for desserts, hot chocolate, pies, or any other treats.
9. Storage:
    - If you have leftovers, store the cinnamon whipped cream in an airtight container in the refrigerator for up to 24 hours. Before serving again, gently whisk by hand to fluff it up.
10. Enjoy:
    - Serve your homemade cinnamon whipped cream and enjoy the warm, spiced flavor it adds to your favorite dishes and drinks!

This cinnamon whipped cream is a delicious way to elevate simple desserts and beverages with its subtle spice and creamy texture. Adjust the sweetness and cinnamon flavor to suit your taste preferences for a personalized touch.

Cinnamon Plum Tart

Ingredients:

For the tart crust:

- 1 1/4 cups all-purpose flour
- 1/2 cup unsalted butter, cold and cut into small pieces
- 1/4 cup granulated sugar
- 1/4 tsp salt
- 1 large egg yolk
- 1-2 tbsp ice water, as needed

For the filling:

- 5-6 ripe plums, pitted and sliced (about 2 cups sliced)
- 1/4 cup granulated sugar (adjust to taste, depending on plum sweetness)
- 1 tbsp cornstarch
- 1/2 tsp ground cinnamon
- 1/4 tsp vanilla extract

For topping:

- 1 tbsp granulated sugar (for sprinkling)
- 1/4 tsp ground cinnamon (for sprinkling)

Instructions:

1. Prepare the tart crust:
    - In a food processor, combine the flour, granulated sugar, and salt. Pulse to mix.
    - Add the cold butter pieces and pulse until the mixture resembles coarse crumbs.
    - Add the egg yolk and 1 tablespoon of ice water at a time, pulsing until the dough just begins to come together. You may need to add an additional tablespoon of ice water if the dough is too dry.
    - Turn the dough out onto a clean surface and gently knead it a few times until it forms a smooth ball. Flatten into a disk, wrap in plastic wrap, and refrigerate for at least 30 minutes.
2. Preheat the oven:
    - Preheat your oven to 375°F (190°C).
3. Prepare the filling:
    - In a large bowl, toss the sliced plums with granulated sugar, cornstarch, ground cinnamon, and vanilla extract until well coated. Set aside.
4. Roll out the dough:
    - On a lightly floured surface, roll out the chilled dough into a circle about 12 inches in diameter. Carefully transfer the dough to a 9-inch tart pan with a

removable bottom. Press the dough into the bottom and sides of the pan, trimming any excess dough.
5. Assemble the tart:
   - Arrange the plum slices in an even layer over the prepared tart crust.
6. Bake the tart:
   - In a small bowl, mix together 1 tablespoon of granulated sugar and 1/4 teaspoon of ground cinnamon. Sprinkle this mixture evenly over the plum slices.
   - Place the tart on a baking sheet (to catch any drips) and bake in the preheated oven for 35-40 minutes, or until the crust is golden brown and the plums are tender.
7. Cool and serve:
   - Allow the Cinnamon Plum Tart to cool slightly in the pan before removing the sides of the tart pan. Serve warm or at room temperature.
8. Optional garnish:
   - For an extra touch, you can dust the tart with powdered sugar before serving.
9. Enjoy:
   - Serve slices of the Cinnamon Plum Tart on its own or with a dollop of whipped cream or vanilla ice cream, if desired.

This Cinnamon Plum Tart is a delightful dessert that showcases the natural sweetness of plums enhanced by the warmth of cinnamon, all nestled in a buttery tart crust. It's perfect for showcasing seasonal fruits and making a memorable treat for any occasion.

Cinnamon Pistachio Biscotti

Ingredients:

- 2 cups all-purpose flour
- 1 cup granulated sugar
- 1/2 cup unsalted butter, softened
- 2 large eggs
- 1 tsp vanilla extract
- 1 tsp ground cinnamon
- 1 tsp baking powder
- 1/4 tsp salt
- 1 cup shelled pistachios, roughly chopped

For optional drizzle:

- 1/2 cup white chocolate chips or melting wafers
- 1/2 tsp vegetable oil

Instructions:

1. Preheat oven and prepare baking sheet:
    - Preheat your oven to 350°F (175°C). Line a baking sheet with parchment paper or a silicone baking mat.
2. Cream butter and sugar:
    - In a large mixing bowl, cream together the softened butter and granulated sugar until light and fluffy.
3. Add eggs and vanilla:
    - Beat in the eggs one at a time, followed by the vanilla extract, mixing well after each addition.
4. Combine dry ingredients:
    - In a separate bowl, whisk together the flour, ground cinnamon, baking powder, and salt.
5. Mix wet and dry ingredients:
    - Gradually add the dry ingredients to the butter-sugar mixture, mixing until just combined. Fold in the chopped pistachios until evenly distributed.
6. Form dough:
    - Divide the dough in half. On a lightly floured surface, shape each half into a log about 12 inches long and 1 1/2 inches wide. Place the logs on the prepared baking sheet, leaving space between them.
7. Bake first bake:
    - Bake in the preheated oven for 25-30 minutes, or until the logs are lightly golden and firm to the touch.
8. Cool and slice:

- Remove the baking sheet from the oven and let the logs cool for about 10-15 minutes. Reduce the oven temperature to 325°F (160°C).

9. Slice biscotti:
    - Using a sharp knife, slice the logs diagonally into 1/2-inch thick slices. Arrange the slices cut-side down on the baking sheet.
10. Second bake:
    - Bake the biscotti for an additional 10-12 minutes, or until the edges are lightly golden and the biscotti are crisp. Flip the biscotti halfway through baking to ensure even baking.
11. Optional drizzle:
    - If desired, melt the white chocolate chips or melting wafers with vegetable oil in the microwave or using a double boiler. Drizzle the melted chocolate over the cooled biscotti.
12. Cool and store:
    - Let the Cinnamon Pistachio Biscotti cool completely on a wire rack. Once cooled, store them in an airtight container at room temperature for up to 2 weeks.
13. Enjoy:
    - Serve the Cinnamon Pistachio Biscotti with a cup of coffee or tea for a delightful treat, or package them up as a homemade gift.

This recipe yields crunchy biscotti with a delightful combination of cinnamon and pistachio flavors, making them perfect for dipping into your favorite hot beverage or enjoying as a standalone snack. Adjust the sweetness or add more cinnamon according to your taste preferences for a personalized touch.

Cinnamon Orange Rolls

Ingredients:

For the dough:

- 4 cups all-purpose flour
- 1/3 cup granulated sugar
- 1 tsp salt
- 1 packet (2 1/4 tsp) active dry yeast
- 3/4 cup milk, warmed to about 110°F (45°C)
- 1/4 cup unsalted butter, melted
- 2 large eggs

For the filling:

- 1/2 cup unsalted butter, softened
- 1 cup packed brown sugar
- Zest of 2 oranges
- 1 tbsp ground cinnamon

For the orange glaze:

- 1 1/2 cups powdered sugar
- 3-4 tbsp freshly squeezed orange juice
- Zest of 1 orange
- 1/2 tsp vanilla extract

Instructions:

1. Make the dough:
    - In a large mixing bowl, combine 3 cups of flour, granulated sugar, salt, and yeast. Mix well.
    - In a separate bowl, whisk together the warmed milk, melted butter, and eggs.
    - Gradually add the wet ingredients to the dry ingredients, stirring until a soft dough forms.
    - Gradually add the remaining 1 cup of flour, 1/4 cup at a time, until the dough is smooth and elastic. You may not need to use all of the flour.
2. Knead the dough:
    - Turn the dough out onto a lightly floured surface and knead for about 5-7 minutes, or until the dough is smooth and elastic.
3. First rise:
    - Place the dough in a greased bowl, turning once to coat. Cover with a clean kitchen towel or plastic wrap and let it rise in a warm, draft-free place for about 1 hour, or until doubled in size.
4. Make the filling:

- In a medium bowl, combine the softened butter, brown sugar, orange zest, and ground cinnamon. Mix until well combined. Set aside.
5. Roll out the dough:
   - Punch down the dough to release the air. On a lightly floured surface, roll out the dough into a rectangle about 12x18 inches.
6. Add the filling:
   - Spread the cinnamon orange filling evenly over the dough, leaving a small border around the edges.
7. Roll up the dough:
   - Starting from one long edge, tightly roll up the dough into a log. Pinch the seam to seal.
8. Slice into rolls:
   - Using a sharp knife or dental floss, cut the log into 12 equal slices.
9. Second rise:
   - Place the rolls in a greased 9x13-inch baking dish or two 9-inch round cake pans. Cover loosely with a kitchen towel and let them rise in a warm place for about 30 minutes, or until puffy.
10. Preheat the oven:
    - Meanwhile, preheat your oven to 350°F (175°C).
11. Bake the rolls:
    - Bake the rolls in the preheated oven for 25-30 minutes, or until they are golden brown.
12. Make the orange glaze:
    - While the rolls are baking, prepare the orange glaze. In a small bowl, whisk together the powdered sugar, freshly squeezed orange juice, orange zest, and vanilla extract until smooth.
13. Glaze the rolls:
    - Remove the rolls from the oven and let them cool in the pan for a few minutes. Drizzle the orange glaze over the warm rolls.
14. Serve:
    - Serve the Cinnamon Orange Rolls warm. Enjoy the delicious combination of citrusy orange flavor with sweet cinnamon rolls!

These Cinnamon Orange Rolls are perfect for breakfast or brunch, and they're sure to be a hit with family and friends. The bright citrus zest and juice in both the filling and the glaze add a refreshing twist to the classic cinnamon roll recipe.

Cinnamon Mint Tea

Ingredients:

- 4 cups water
- 1 cinnamon stick
- 1/4 cup fresh mint leaves (or 2-3 mint tea bags)
- Honey or sugar, to taste (optional)

Instructions:

1. Boil the water:
   - In a medium-sized saucepan, bring 4 cups of water to a boil.
2. Add cinnamon and mint:
   - Once the water boils, add 1 cinnamon stick and 1/4 cup of fresh mint leaves (or mint tea bags) to the boiling water.
3. Steep the tea:
   - Turn off the heat and let the cinnamon and mint steep in the hot water for about 5-10 minutes, depending on how strong you prefer your tea. Cover the saucepan with a lid during steeping to keep the flavors intact.
4. Strain the tea:
   - After steeping, remove the cinnamon stick and mint leaves (or tea bags) from the saucepan using a slotted spoon or by straining the liquid into a teapot or serving pitcher.
5. Sweeten (optional):
   - If desired, sweeten the tea with honey or sugar to taste. Stir until the sweetener is dissolved.
6. Serve:
   - Pour the Cinnamon Mint Tea into cups and serve it hot.
7. Enjoy:
   - Savor the soothing blend of cinnamon and mint flavors in this comforting herbal tea. It's perfect for warming up on chilly days or as a refreshing drink to relax with any time of day.

Cinnamon Mint Tea offers a delightful combination of herbal notes with a hint of sweetness from the cinnamon. Adjust the steeping time and sweetness level to suit your taste preferences for a personalized tea experience.

Cinnamon Pineapple Upside-Down Cake

Ingredients:

For the topping:

- 1/4 cup unsalted butter
- 3/4 cup packed light brown sugar
- 1/2 tsp ground cinnamon
- 1 can (20 oz) pineapple slices in juice, drained (reserve juice)
- Maraschino cherries, for garnish (optional)

For the cake batter:

- 1 1/2 cups all-purpose flour
- 1 1/2 tsp baking powder
- 1/4 tsp salt
- 1/2 tsp ground cinnamon
- 1/2 cup unsalted butter, softened
- 3/4 cup granulated sugar
- 2 large eggs
- 1 tsp vanilla extract
- 1/2 cup reserved pineapple juice (from the can)
- 1/4 cup milk

Instructions:

1. Preheat oven:
   - Preheat your oven to 350°F (175°C). Grease a 9-inch round cake pan.
2. Make the topping:
   - In a small saucepan, melt 1/4 cup of unsalted butter over medium heat.
   - Stir in the packed light brown sugar and ground cinnamon until the sugar is dissolved and the mixture is smooth.
   - Pour the mixture into the prepared cake pan, spreading it evenly over the bottom.
   - Arrange the drained pineapple slices over the brown sugar mixture in a single layer. You can place a maraschino cherry in the center of each pineapple slice if desired.
3. Make the cake batter:
   - In a medium bowl, whisk together the all-purpose flour, baking powder, salt, and ground cinnamon until well combined.
   - In a large mixing bowl, beat 1/2 cup of softened unsalted butter with 3/4 cup of granulated sugar until light and fluffy.
   - Add the eggs one at a time, beating well after each addition. Mix in the vanilla extract.

- Gradually add the dry flour mixture to the butter-sugar mixture, alternating with the reserved pineapple juice and milk. Begin and end with the dry ingredients, mixing until just combined after each addition. Be careful not to overmix.
4. Assemble and bake:
    - Carefully spread the cake batter over the pineapple slices and brown sugar mixture in the cake pan, smoothing the top with a spatula.
    - Bake in the preheated oven for 40-45 minutes, or until a toothpick inserted into the center of the cake comes out clean.
5. Cool and invert:
    - Remove the cake from the oven and let it cool in the pan on a wire rack for 10-15 minutes.
    - Place a serving plate upside down over the cake pan. Using oven mitts, carefully invert the cake onto the serving plate. Gently lift off the cake pan.
6. Serve:
    - Serve the Cinnamon Pineapple Upside-Down Cake warm or at room temperature. Enjoy the delicious combination of caramelized pineapple, cinnamon-spiced cake, and sweet brown sugar topping!

This Cinnamon Pineapple Upside-Down Cake is a wonderful dessert that combines tropical flavors with warm cinnamon spice, making it perfect for any occasion or as a delightful treat with afternoon tea. Adjust the sweetness or cinnamon flavor to suit your taste preferences for a personalized touch.

Cinnamon Mocha Brownies

Ingredients:

- 1/2 cup unsalted butter
- 1 cup granulated sugar
- 2 large eggs
- 1 tsp vanilla extract
- 1/2 cup all-purpose flour
- 1/3 cup unsweetened cocoa powder
- 1/4 tsp salt
- 1/2 tsp ground cinnamon
- 1/2 cup semisweet chocolate chips or chunks
- 1/4 cup brewed coffee or espresso, cooled

For the cinnamon mocha glaze:

- 1/2 cup powdered sugar
- 1 tbsp unsweetened cocoa powder
- 1/4 tsp ground cinnamon
- 1-2 tbsp brewed coffee or espresso

Instructions:

1. Preheat oven:
    - Preheat your oven to 350°F (175°C). Grease or line an 8x8-inch baking pan with parchment paper.
2. Prepare the brownie batter:
    - In a microwave-safe bowl, melt the unsalted butter in the microwave in 30-second intervals until completely melted.
    - Stir in the granulated sugar until well combined.
    - Add the eggs one at a time, mixing well after each addition.
    - Mix in the vanilla extract.
3. Add dry ingredients:
    - In a separate bowl, whisk together the all-purpose flour, unsweetened cocoa powder, salt, and ground cinnamon.
    - Gradually add the dry ingredients to the wet ingredients, mixing until just combined.
4. Add coffee and chocolate:
    - Stir in the brewed coffee or espresso until smooth.
    - Fold in the semisweet chocolate chips or chunks until evenly distributed in the batter.
5. Bake the brownies:
    - Pour the brownie batter into the prepared baking pan, spreading it evenly with a spatula.

- Bake in the preheated oven for 25-30 minutes, or until a toothpick inserted into the center comes out with moist crumbs. Do not overbake.
6. Make the cinnamon mocha glaze:
    - While the brownies are baking, prepare the cinnamon mocha glaze.
    - In a small bowl, whisk together the powdered sugar, unsweetened cocoa powder, and ground cinnamon.
    - Gradually add 1-2 tablespoons of brewed coffee or espresso, stirring until smooth and the desired glaze consistency is reached.
7. Glaze the brownies:
    - Once the brownies are done baking and have cooled slightly (but are still warm), drizzle the cinnamon mocha glaze over the top using a spoon or spatula.
8. Cool and serve:
    - Let the brownies cool completely in the pan on a wire rack before cutting into squares.
9. Enjoy:
    - Serve the Cinnamon Mocha Brownies as a delicious dessert or treat. The combination of chocolate, coffee, and cinnamon flavors makes these brownies a delightful indulgence!

These Cinnamon Mocha Brownies are sure to satisfy your sweet tooth with their rich and aromatic flavors. They are perfect for sharing with friends and family or enjoying with a cup of coffee for a delightful afternoon treat. Adjust the intensity of the coffee and cinnamon to suit your taste preferences for a personalized brownie experience.

Cinnamon Raspberry Smoothie

Ingredients:

- 1 cup frozen raspberries
- 1 ripe banana, peeled and frozen
- 1 cup almond milk (or any milk of your choice)
- 1/2 tsp ground cinnamon
- 1 tbsp honey or maple syrup (optional, for added sweetness)
- Ice cubes (optional, for a thicker smoothie)

Instructions:

1. Prepare the ingredients:
   - Ensure that your raspberries are frozen and your banana is peeled and frozen beforehand for a chilled smoothie.
2. Blend:
   - In a blender, combine the frozen raspberries, frozen banana, almond milk, ground cinnamon, and honey or maple syrup (if using).
3. Blend until smooth:
   - Blend all the ingredients together until smooth and creamy. If you prefer a thicker smoothie, you can add a handful of ice cubes and blend again until smooth.
4. Taste and adjust:
   - Taste the smoothie and adjust the sweetness by adding more honey or maple syrup if desired.
5. Serve:
   - Pour the Cinnamon Raspberry Smoothie into glasses and serve immediately.
6. Optional garnish:
   - Garnish with a few fresh raspberries or a sprinkle of ground cinnamon on top for an extra touch.
7. Enjoy:
   - Enjoy this refreshing and nutritious Cinnamon Raspberry Smoothie as a breakfast drink, snack, or post-workout refresher!

This smoothie is not only delicious but also packed with antioxidants from the raspberries and potassium from the banana. The addition of cinnamon adds a warm, comforting flavor that complements the fruity tang of the raspberries beautifully. Adjust the ingredients to suit your taste preferences and enjoy this healthy treat any time of day!

Cinnamon Steak Rub

Ingredients:

- 2 tbsp ground cinnamon
- 2 tbsp paprika
- 1 tbsp garlic powder
- 1 tbsp onion powder
- 1 tbsp ground black pepper
- 1 tbsp kosher salt
- 1 tsp ground cumin
- 1/2 tsp cayenne pepper (adjust to taste for spiciness)
- 1/4 cup brown sugar (optional, for a slightly sweet flavor)

Instructions:

1. Mix the spices:
    - In a small bowl, combine the ground cinnamon, paprika, garlic powder, onion powder, black pepper, kosher salt, ground cumin, and cayenne pepper.
2. Optional sweetener:
    - If you prefer a slightly sweet flavor, you can add brown sugar to the spice mixture. Adjust the amount to your taste preferences.
3. Rub the steak:
    - Pat the steaks dry with paper towels to remove excess moisture. Rub the cinnamon steak rub generously over both sides of the steaks, pressing it into the meat to adhere.
4. Let it sit:
    - Let the seasoned steaks sit at room temperature for about 15-20 minutes before cooking. This allows the flavors to penetrate the meat.
5. Cooking methods:
    - Grill: Preheat your grill to medium-high heat. Grill the steaks according to your preferred level of doneness, flipping once halfway through cooking.
    - Pan-sear: Heat a heavy skillet over medium-high heat. Add a bit of oil or butter to the pan and cook the steaks for a few minutes on each side until browned and cooked to your liking.
    - Oven: Preheat your oven to 400°F (200°C). Sear the steaks in a hot skillet for 2-3 minutes per side, then transfer the skillet to the oven to finish cooking to your desired doneness.
6. Rest and serve:
    - Once cooked, let the steaks rest for a few minutes before slicing or serving. This allows the juices to redistribute within the meat for a juicier steak.
7. Enjoy:
    - Serve your deliciously flavored cinnamon steak alongside your favorite side dishes. The cinnamon steak rub adds a warm, aromatic flavor that complements the richness of the steak.

This Cinnamon Steak Rub is versatile and adds a unique twist to your steak dinners. Adjust the amount of spices and sweetness according to your taste preferences. It's sure to impress your family and guests with its flavorful combination of spices!

Cinnamon Pesto Pasta

Ingredients:

For the pesto:

- 2 cups fresh basil leaves, packed
- 1/2 cup grated Parmesan cheese
- 1/2 cup pine nuts or walnuts
- 2 cloves garlic, peeled
- 1/2 tsp ground cinnamon
- 1/2 cup extra virgin olive oil
- Salt and freshly ground black pepper, to taste

For the pasta:

- 12 oz (about 340g) pasta of your choice (such as spaghetti, fettuccine, or penne)
- Salt, for cooking pasta
- Grated Parmesan cheese, for serving (optional)
- Fresh basil leaves, for garnish (optional)

Instructions:

1. Make the pesto:
    - In a food processor, combine the basil leaves, grated Parmesan cheese, pine nuts (or walnuts), garlic cloves, and ground cinnamon.
    - Pulse several times until the ingredients are coarsely chopped.
    - With the food processor running, gradually add the olive oil in a steady stream until the pesto is smooth and well combined. You may need to stop and scrape down the sides of the food processor with a spatula.
    - Season the pesto with salt and freshly ground black pepper to taste. Adjust the amount of cinnamon according to your preference for a subtle or more pronounced flavor.
2. Cook the pasta:
    - Bring a large pot of salted water to a boil. Cook the pasta according to the package instructions until al dente.
    - Reserve about 1/2 cup of the pasta cooking water, then drain the pasta.
3. Combine the pesto and pasta:
    - In a large mixing bowl or the pot used to cook the pasta, toss the drained pasta with the prepared cinnamon pesto.
    - Add a little of the reserved pasta cooking water as needed to loosen the pesto and coat the pasta evenly. The starchy pasta water helps to create a creamy sauce.
4. Serve:
    - Divide the Cinnamon Pesto Pasta among serving plates or bowls.

- If desired, sprinkle grated Parmesan cheese over each serving and garnish with fresh basil leaves.
5. Enjoy:
    - Serve the Cinnamon Pesto Pasta immediately, while it's still warm, and enjoy the unique combination of flavors from the basil pesto with the subtle warmth of cinnamon.

This Cinnamon Pesto Pasta is a delightful twist on traditional pesto pasta dishes, offering a comforting and aromatic experience. It's perfect for a quick weeknight dinner or a special meal with friends and family. Adjust the ingredients and seasonings according to your taste preferences for a personalized pasta dish that's sure to impress!

Cinnamon Chicken Curry

Ingredients:

- 1 1/2 lbs (680g) boneless, skinless chicken thighs or breasts, cut into bite-sized pieces
- 2 tbsp vegetable oil or ghee
- 1 large onion, finely chopped
- 4 cloves garlic, minced
- 1-inch piece of ginger, grated or minced
- 1 cinnamon stick
- 2 bay leaves
- 1 tsp ground turmeric
- 1 tsp ground cumin
- 1 tsp ground coriander
- 1/2 tsp ground cinnamon
- 1/2 tsp ground cardamom
- 1/4 tsp cayenne pepper (adjust to taste)
- 1 can (14 oz / 400ml) diced tomatoes
- 1 can (14 oz / 400ml) coconut milk
- Salt and pepper, to taste
- Fresh cilantro, chopped (for garnish)
- Cooked rice or naan bread, for serving

Instructions:

1. Prepare the chicken:
    - Season the chicken pieces with salt and pepper.
2. Sear the chicken:
    - In a large skillet or Dutch oven, heat 1 tablespoon of vegetable oil or ghee over medium-high heat.
    - Add the chicken pieces in batches and cook until browned on all sides, about 5-7 minutes. Remove the chicken from the skillet and set aside.
3. Make the curry base:
    - In the same skillet, add another tablespoon of oil if needed.
    - Add the chopped onion and cook until softened, about 5 minutes.
    - Add the minced garlic, grated ginger, cinnamon stick, and bay leaves. Cook for another 2 minutes until fragrant.
4. Add spices:
    - Stir in the ground turmeric, ground cumin, ground coriander, ground cinnamon, ground cardamom, and cayenne pepper. Cook for 1 minute, stirring constantly.
5. Simmer the curry:
    - Pour in the diced tomatoes with their juices and coconut milk. Stir to combine.
    - Bring the mixture to a simmer, then reduce the heat to low.
6. Add chicken and simmer:

- Return the seared chicken pieces to the skillet, along with any juices that have accumulated.
            - Cover and simmer gently for 20-25 minutes, or until the chicken is cooked through and tender, and the flavors have melded together.
     7. Adjust seasoning:
            - Taste and adjust the seasoning with salt and pepper, as needed.
     8. Serve:
            - Remove the cinnamon stick and bay leaves from the curry.
            - Serve the Cinnamon Chicken Curry hot, garnished with fresh chopped cilantro, alongside cooked rice or warm naan bread.
     9. Enjoy:
            - Enjoy this flavorful and aromatic Cinnamon Chicken Curry as a comforting meal. The combination of spices and coconut milk creates a rich and creamy sauce that pairs perfectly with rice or naan bread.

This Cinnamon Chicken Curry is a delicious twist on traditional curry dishes, offering a unique blend of spices that adds warmth and depth to the dish. Adjust the level of cayenne pepper according to your spice preference, and feel free to customize with additional vegetables or garnishes as desired.

Cinnamon Lentil Soup

Ingredients:

- 1 cup dried lentils (green or brown), rinsed and drained
- 1 onion, finely chopped
- 2 cloves garlic, minced
- 1 carrot, diced
- 1 celery stalk, diced
- 1 can (14 oz / 400g) diced tomatoes
- 4 cups vegetable or chicken broth
- 1 cinnamon stick
- 1 tsp ground cumin
- 1/2 tsp ground coriander
- 1/2 tsp ground cinnamon
- 1/4 tsp ground turmeric
- Pinch of cayenne pepper (optional, for heat)
- Salt and pepper, to taste
- 2 tbsp olive oil
- Fresh parsley or cilantro, chopped (for garnish)
- Lemon wedges (for serving)

Instructions:

1. Prepare the lentils:
   - Rinse the dried lentils under cold water and drain them thoroughly.
2. Sauté aromatics:
   - In a large pot or Dutch oven, heat the olive oil over medium heat.
   - Add the chopped onion, garlic, carrot, and celery. Sauté for about 5-7 minutes until the vegetables are softened and aromatic.
3. Add spices:
   - Stir in the ground cumin, ground coriander, ground cinnamon, ground turmeric, and a pinch of cayenne pepper (if using). Cook for 1 minute until the spices are fragrant.
4. Simmer soup:
   - Add the rinsed lentils, diced tomatoes (with their juices), vegetable or chicken broth, and the cinnamon stick to the pot. Stir to combine.
5. Cook lentil soup:
   - Bring the soup to a boil, then reduce the heat to low. Cover and simmer gently for about 25-30 minutes, or until the lentils are tender and cooked through.
6. Season and adjust:
   - Season the Cinnamon Lentil Soup with salt and pepper, to taste. Adjust the spices if desired, adding more cinnamon or cayenne pepper according to your preference.
7. Serve:

       - Remove the cinnamon stick from the soup before serving.
       - Ladle the hot soup into bowls and garnish with fresh chopped parsley or cilantro.
       - Serve with lemon wedges on the side for squeezing over the soup, if desired.
8. Enjoy:
       - Enjoy this comforting and nutritious Cinnamon Lentil Soup as a satisfying meal. The combination of lentils, warming spices, and vegetables makes it perfect for chilly days.

This Cinnamon Lentil Soup is versatile and can be customized with additional vegetables or herbs. It's a great option for a wholesome lunch or dinner, providing plenty of protein and fiber from the lentils along with rich flavors from the spices. Adjust the consistency by adding more broth if needed and serve it alongside crusty bread for a complete meal.

Cinnamon Garlic Shrimp

Ingredients:

- 1 lb (450g) large shrimp, peeled and deveined
- 4 cloves garlic, minced
- 1/2 tsp ground cinnamon
- 1/4 tsp paprika
- Salt and pepper, to taste
- 2 tbsp olive oil
- 2 tbsp butter
- Fresh parsley, chopped (for garnish)
- Lemon wedges (for serving)

Instructions:

1. Prepare the shrimp:
    - Pat the shrimp dry with paper towels and season with salt, pepper, ground cinnamon, and paprika. Toss to coat the shrimp evenly.
2. Heat the pan:
    - In a large skillet, heat olive oil and butter over medium-high heat until the butter is melted and the skillet is hot.
3. Sauté the shrimp:
    - Add the minced garlic to the skillet and sauté for about 30 seconds until fragrant.
4. Cook the shrimp:
    - Add the seasoned shrimp to the skillet in a single layer. Cook for 2-3 minutes on each side, or until the shrimp are pink and opaque. Be careful not to overcook them.
5. Finish and garnish:
    - Once the shrimp are cooked through, remove the skillet from the heat.
    - Sprinkle fresh chopped parsley over the shrimp for garnish.
6. Serve:
    - Transfer the Cinnamon Garlic Shrimp to a serving plate or dish.
    - Serve immediately with lemon wedges on the side for squeezing over the shrimp.
7. Enjoy:
    - Enjoy the Cinnamon Garlic Shrimp as a delicious appetizer or main dish. The combination of cinnamon and garlic enhances the natural sweetness of the shrimp, creating a flavorful and aromatic dish.

This recipe is quick and easy to prepare, making it perfect for a weeknight dinner or as a party appetizer. Serve the shrimp over rice or pasta, or enjoy them on their own with a side of vegetables for a light and satisfying meal. Adjust the amount of cinnamon and garlic to suit your taste preferences and enjoy the delightful flavors of this Cinnamon Garlic Shrimp dish!

Cinnamon Lamb Kebabs

Ingredients:

- 1 lb (450g) lamb shoulder or leg, cubed
- 2 cloves garlic, minced
- 1 tsp ground cinnamon
- 1 tsp ground cumin
- 1/2 tsp ground coriander
- 1/2 tsp ground paprika
- 1/4 tsp ground turmeric
- 1/4 tsp cayenne pepper (optional, for heat)
- 2 tbsp olive oil
- Juice of 1 lemon
- Salt and pepper, to taste
- Skewers (if using wooden skewers, soak them in water for 30 minutes before using)
- Fresh parsley or cilantro, chopped (for garnish)
- Lemon wedges (for serving)

Instructions:

1. Marinate the lamb:
    - In a bowl, combine the cubed lamb with minced garlic, ground cinnamon, ground cumin, ground coriander, ground paprika, ground turmeric, cayenne pepper (if using), olive oil, and lemon juice. Season with salt and pepper to taste. Mix well to coat the lamb evenly. Cover and refrigerate for at least 1 hour, or overnight for best flavor.
2. Skewer the lamb:
    - Preheat the grill to medium-high heat. If using wooden skewers, make sure they are soaked in water for 30 minutes to prevent burning.
    - Thread the marinated lamb cubes onto the skewers, leaving a little space between each piece.
3. Grill the kebabs:
    - Brush the grill grates with oil to prevent sticking. Place the lamb kebabs on the grill and cook for about 8-10 minutes, turning occasionally, or until the lamb is cooked to your desired doneness and has nice grill marks.
4. Rest and garnish:
    - Remove the Cinnamon Lamb Kebabs from the grill and let them rest for a few minutes.
    - Sprinkle chopped fresh parsley or cilantro over the kebabs for garnish.
5. Serve:
    - Serve the Cinnamon Lamb Kebabs hot, accompanied by lemon wedges on the side for squeezing over the meat.
6. Enjoy:

- Enjoy these flavorful and tender Cinnamon Lamb Kebabs as a main dish with your favorite sides, such as rice, grilled vegetables, or salad.

This recipe brings out the natural sweetness of lamb while adding a warm and aromatic touch with cinnamon and other spices. Adjust the amount of cayenne pepper for a spicier kick or omit it altogether for a milder flavor. These kebabs are perfect for grilling outdoors or cooking indoors on a grill pan, bringing a taste of Mediterranean cuisine to your table.

Cinnamon Chili

Ingredients:

- 1 lb (450g) ground beef or turkey
- 1 onion, diced
- 2 cloves garlic, minced
- 1 bell pepper, diced (any color)
- 1 can (14 oz / 400g) diced tomatoes
- 1 can (15 oz / 425g) kidney beans, drained and rinsed
- 1 can (15 oz / 425g) black beans, drained and rinsed
- 2 cups beef or vegetable broth
- 2 tbsp tomato paste
- 1 tbsp chili powder
- 1 tsp ground cumin
- 1/2 tsp ground cinnamon
- 1/2 tsp paprika
- 1/4 tsp cayenne pepper (adjust to taste)
- Salt and pepper, to taste
- 2 tbsp olive oil
- Fresh cilantro or parsley, chopped (for garnish)
- Sour cream or shredded cheese (optional, for serving)

Instructions:

1. Brown the meat:
    - In a large pot or Dutch oven, heat olive oil over medium-high heat. Add the ground beef or turkey and cook until browned, breaking it up with a spoon as it cooks.
2. Sauté aromatics:
    - Add diced onion, minced garlic, and diced bell pepper to the pot. Cook for 5-7 minutes, until the vegetables are softened and aromatic.
3. Add spices and tomato paste:
    - Stir in chili powder, ground cumin, ground cinnamon, paprika, and cayenne pepper (if using). Cook for 1 minute, stirring constantly.
    - Add tomato paste and cook for another minute, stirring to coat the meat and vegetables.
4. Simmer the chili:
    - Pour in diced tomatoes (with their juices), kidney beans, black beans, and beef or vegetable broth. Stir well to combine.
    - Bring the chili to a boil, then reduce the heat to low. Cover and simmer for 30-40 minutes, stirring occasionally, until the chili has thickened and flavors have melded together.
5. Season and adjust:

- Taste the chili and season with salt and pepper as needed. Adjust the level of cayenne pepper for more or less heat.
6. Serve:
    - Ladle the Cinnamon Chili into bowls.
    - Garnish with chopped fresh cilantro or parsley.
    - Serve hot, optionally topped with sour cream or shredded cheese.
7. Enjoy:
    - Enjoy this comforting and flavorful Cinnamon Chili on its own or with your favorite toppings. The addition of cinnamon adds a subtle warmth and complexity to the dish, making it a delicious twist on classic chili.

This Cinnamon Chili recipe is versatile and can be customized with additional vegetables or beans according to your preference. It's perfect for feeding a crowd or meal prepping for easy lunches throughout the week. Serve with cornbread or crusty bread for a complete and satisfying meal.

Cinnamon Cornbread Stuffing

Ingredients:

- 1 batch of cornbread (8x8-inch pan), cooled and cut into cubes (homemade or store-bought)
- 6 tbsp unsalted butter
- 1 onion, finely chopped
- 2 celery stalks, finely chopped
- 2 cloves garlic, minced
- 1 tsp ground cinnamon
- 1/2 tsp ground sage
- 1/2 tsp dried thyme
- Salt and pepper, to taste
- 1/2 cup chicken or vegetable broth, plus more if needed
- 1/2 cup dried cranberries or chopped dried apricots (optional)
- Fresh parsley or sage, chopped (for garnish, optional)

Instructions:

1. Prepare the cornbread:
    - Prepare your cornbread according to the recipe or package instructions. Let it cool completely, then cut it into cubes. You can make the cornbread a day ahead for easier preparation.
2. Sauté vegetables:
    - In a large skillet or frying pan, melt the butter over medium heat. Add the chopped onion and celery, and cook until softened, about 5-7 minutes.
3. Add seasonings:
    - Stir in the minced garlic, ground cinnamon, ground sage, dried thyme, salt, and pepper. Cook for 1-2 minutes until fragrant.
4. Combine with cornbread:
    - Transfer the sautéed vegetables and seasonings to a large mixing bowl with the cubed cornbread.
5. Moisten with broth:
    - Gradually pour the chicken or vegetable broth over the cornbread mixture, tossing gently to combine. Add more broth if needed to moisten the stuffing to your desired consistency. The cornbread should be moist but not soggy.
6. Add optional ingredients:
    - If using dried cranberries or chopped dried apricots, add them to the cornbread stuffing mixture and toss gently to distribute evenly.
7. Bake the stuffing:
    - Preheat your oven to 350°F (175°C).
    - Transfer the cinnamon cornbread stuffing mixture to a greased baking dish. Cover with foil and bake for 30 minutes.
8. Finish baking:

- Remove the foil and bake for an additional 10-15 minutes, or until the top of the stuffing is lightly golden and crisp.
9. Garnish and serve:
    - Remove the Cinnamon Cornbread Stuffing from the oven and let it rest for a few minutes.
    - Garnish with chopped fresh parsley or sage, if desired, before serving.
10. Enjoy:
    - Serve the Cinnamon Cornbread Stuffing warm as a delicious side dish for Thanksgiving, Christmas, or any festive meal. It pairs well with roast turkey, chicken, or pork.

This Cinnamon Cornbread Stuffing recipe adds a subtle warmth and sweetness to the traditional stuffing, making it a flavorful addition to your holiday table. Adjust the seasonings and add-ins according to your taste preferences. It's sure to be a hit with family and friends!

Cinnamon Bacon Wrapped Dates

Ingredients:

- 16 Medjool dates, pitted
- 8 slices of bacon, cut in half crosswise
- 1 tsp ground cinnamon
- Toothpicks or wooden skewers

Instructions:

1. Prepare the dates:
    - Preheat your oven to 375°F (190°C).
    - Slice each Medjool date lengthwise on one side to remove the pit. Be careful not to cut all the way through the date.
2. Stuff the dates:
    - In a small bowl, mix the ground cinnamon.
    - Sprinkle a pinch of ground cinnamon into each date cavity.
3. Wrap with bacon:
    - Take a half-slice of bacon and wrap it around each stuffed date, securing it with a toothpick or wooden skewer through the center. Place the bacon seam-side down on a baking sheet lined with parchment paper.
4. Bake the dates:
    - Arrange the bacon-wrapped dates on the baking sheet in a single layer.
    - Bake in the preheated oven for 15-20 minutes, or until the bacon is crispy and cooked through. You may want to turn the dates halfway through baking for even cooking.
5. Serve:
    - Remove the Cinnamon Bacon Wrapped Dates from the oven and let them cool slightly.
    - Transfer to a serving platter and serve warm.
6. Enjoy:
    - Enjoy these delicious Cinnamon Bacon Wrapped Dates as an appetizer or party snack. The combination of sweet dates, savory bacon, and warm cinnamon makes them irresistible!

These Cinnamon Bacon Wrapped Dates are perfect for entertaining guests or as a tasty treat any time. They offer a delightful balance of flavors and textures that will surely be a hit at your next gathering. Adjust the amount of cinnamon according to your preference for a subtle or more pronounced cinnamon flavor.

Cinnamon BBQ Sauce

Ingredients:

- 1 cup ketchup
- 1/2 cup apple cider vinegar
- 1/4 cup brown sugar
- 2 tbsp honey
- 2 tbsp Worcestershire sauce
- 1 tbsp Dijon mustard
- 1 tsp ground cinnamon
- 1/2 tsp garlic powder
- 1/2 tsp onion powder
- 1/4 tsp smoked paprika
- Salt and pepper, to taste

Instructions:

1. Combine ingredients:
   - In a medium saucepan, combine all the ingredients: ketchup, apple cider vinegar, brown sugar, honey, Worcestershire sauce, Dijon mustard, ground cinnamon, garlic powder, onion powder, smoked paprika, salt, and pepper.
2. Simmer the sauce:
   - Stir the mixture well to combine all the ingredients.
   - Bring the sauce to a simmer over medium heat, stirring frequently to prevent burning.
3. Cook and thicken:
   - Reduce the heat to low and let the sauce simmer gently for about 15-20 minutes, stirring occasionally, until it thickens to your desired consistency. The sauce should coat the back of a spoon.
4. Adjust seasoning:
   - Taste the Cinnamon BBQ Sauce and adjust the seasoning with more salt, pepper, or cinnamon, if desired.
5. Cool and store:
   - Remove the saucepan from the heat and let the Cinnamon BBQ Sauce cool to room temperature.
   - Transfer the sauce to a glass jar or airtight container for storage. Store in the refrigerator for up to 2 weeks.
6. Use:
   - Use the Cinnamon BBQ Sauce as a marinade, glaze, or dipping sauce for grilled meats such as chicken, ribs, or pork. It can also be used as a sauce for burgers or as a flavor boost for roasted vegetables.
7. Enjoy:

- Enjoy the sweet and savory flavors of this Cinnamon BBQ Sauce, enhanced by the warmth of cinnamon. It's perfect for adding a unique twist to your barbecue dishes and impressing your guests with its delicious flavor profile.

This Cinnamon BBQ Sauce recipe is versatile and can be adjusted to suit your taste preferences. Feel free to add more honey for sweetness or adjust the amount of cinnamon for a stronger or milder flavor. Experiment with different dishes to see how this sauce can elevate your cooking!

Cinnamon Sweet Chili Wings

Ingredients:

- 2 lbs (about 1 kg) chicken wings, tips removed and wings separated into drumettes and flats
- 1/2 cup sweet chili sauce
- 2 tbsp soy sauce
- 2 tbsp honey
- 1 tbsp vegetable oil
- 1 tsp ground cinnamon
- 1/2 tsp garlic powder
- Salt and pepper, to taste
- Fresh cilantro or green onions, chopped (for garnish)
- Sesame seeds (optional, for garnish)

Instructions:

1. Marinate the wings:
    - In a large bowl, combine sweet chili sauce, soy sauce, honey, vegetable oil, ground cinnamon, garlic powder, salt, and pepper. Mix well to combine.
2. Coat the wings:
    - Add the chicken wings to the marinade and toss until evenly coated. Cover the bowl with plastic wrap or transfer the wings and marinade to a large zip-top bag. Refrigerate for at least 1 hour, or preferably overnight, to marinate.
3. Preheat the oven:
    - Preheat your oven to 400°F (200°C). Line a baking sheet with aluminum foil and place a wire rack on top.
4. Arrange and bake:
    - Arrange the marinated chicken wings in a single layer on the wire rack. Reserve the marinade.
    - Bake the wings in the preheated oven for 40-45 minutes, flipping halfway through, until they are golden brown and crispy.
5. Prepare the glaze:
    - While the wings are baking, transfer the reserved marinade to a small saucepan. Bring to a simmer over medium heat and cook for about 5-7 minutes, stirring occasionally, until the sauce thickens slightly.
6. Glaze the wings:
    - Once the wings are cooked through and crispy, remove them from the oven. Brush the wings generously with the cinnamon sweet chili glaze.
7. Finish and garnish:
    - Return the glazed wings to the oven and bake for an additional 5 minutes to set the glaze.
8. Serve:

- Remove the Cinnamon Sweet Chili Wings from the oven and transfer them to a serving platter.
- Garnish with chopped fresh cilantro or green onions and sesame seeds, if desired.

9. Enjoy:
    - Serve the Cinnamon Sweet Chili Wings hot as a delicious appetizer or main dish. The combination of sweet chili sauce with a hint of cinnamon creates a flavorful and aromatic dish that is sure to be a crowd-pleaser!

These Cinnamon Sweet Chili Wings are perfect for game day, parties, or any occasion where you want to serve up something a little different and utterly delicious. Adjust the amount of chili sauce and cinnamon to suit your taste preferences, and enjoy these wings with your favorite dipping sauce on the side!

Cinnamon Avocado Toast

Ingredients:

- 2 slices of whole grain bread (or bread of your choice), toasted
- 1 ripe avocado
- Ground cinnamon, to taste
- Honey or maple syrup, for drizzling (optional)
- Salt and pepper, to taste
- Optional toppings: sliced banana, nuts (such as almonds or walnuts), chia seeds, or a sprinkle of granola

Instructions:

1. Prepare the avocado:
   - Cut the avocado in half lengthwise and remove the pit. Scoop out the flesh into a bowl.
2. Mash the avocado:
   - Using a fork, mash the avocado until smooth or leave it slightly chunky, depending on your preference.
3. Season the avocado:
   - Add a pinch of salt and pepper to the mashed avocado, to taste.
4. Assemble the toast:
   - Spread the mashed avocado evenly onto the toasted bread slices.
5. Sprinkle with cinnamon:
   - Sprinkle ground cinnamon over the avocado toast slices, according to your taste preference. Cinnamon adds a warm and sweet flavor that complements the creamy avocado.
6. Optional toppings:
   - For added texture and flavor, you can drizzle a little honey or maple syrup over the cinnamon avocado toast. Alternatively, top with sliced banana, nuts, chia seeds, or granola for extra crunch and nutrition.
7. Serve:
   - Serve the Cinnamon Avocado Toast immediately while the bread is still warm and crispy.
8. Enjoy:
   - Enjoy this wholesome and flavorful Cinnamon Avocado Toast for breakfast, brunch, or as a quick and satisfying snack. It's packed with healthy fats, fiber, and essential nutrients from the avocado and whole grain bread.

Cinnamon Avocado Toast is versatile and can be customized with various toppings to suit your taste preferences and dietary needs. It's a great way to start your day with a nutritious and delicious meal that will keep you energized and satisfied.

Cinnamon Spinach Salad

Ingredients:

- 6 cups fresh spinach leaves, washed and dried
- 1/2 cup pecans or walnuts, toasted
- 1/2 cup dried cranberries or raisins
- 1/4 cup crumbled feta or goat cheese (optional)
- 1 apple, thinly sliced
- 1/4 red onion, thinly sliced

For the Cinnamon Vinaigrette:

- 1/4 cup olive oil
- 2 tablespoons apple cider vinegar
- 1 tablespoon honey
- 1/2 teaspoon ground cinnamon
- Salt and pepper, to taste

Instructions:

1. Prepare the salad:
    - In a large salad bowl, combine the fresh spinach leaves, toasted pecans or walnuts, dried cranberries or raisins, crumbled feta or goat cheese (if using), sliced apple, and red onion. Toss gently to mix.
2. Make the cinnamon vinaigrette:
    - In a small bowl, whisk together the olive oil, apple cider vinegar, honey, ground cinnamon, salt, and pepper until well combined.
3. Dress the salad:
    - Drizzle the cinnamon vinaigrette over the spinach salad. Toss gently to coat the ingredients evenly with the dressing.
4. Serve:
    - Transfer the Cinnamon Spinach Salad to individual serving plates or bowls.
5. Enjoy:
    - Serve the salad immediately as a refreshing and nutritious side dish or main course. The combination of spinach, nuts, fruit, and cheese, dressed with a hint of cinnamon vinaigrette, creates a delicious harmony of flavors and textures.

This Cinnamon Spinach Salad recipe is versatile, and you can adjust the ingredients based on your preferences. It's perfect for any occasion, from a light lunch to a side dish for dinner parties. The cinnamon vinaigrette adds a unique twist to the salad, enhancing its overall appeal and flavor profile.

Cinnamon Sourdough Bread

Ingredients:

- 1 cup active sourdough starter (100% hydration)
- 3 cups bread flour
- 1 cup whole wheat flour
- 1 1/2 cups lukewarm water
- 2 tbsp honey or maple syrup
- 2 tsp ground cinnamon
- 1 1/2 tsp salt
- Optional: 1/2 cup raisins or chopped nuts for added texture and flavor

Instructions:

1. Prepare the dough:
    - In a large mixing bowl, combine the active sourdough starter, lukewarm water, and honey or maple syrup. Mix until well combined.
    - Add the bread flour, whole wheat flour, ground cinnamon, and salt to the bowl. Stir with a wooden spoon or dough whisk until a shaggy dough forms.
2. Knead the dough:
    - Transfer the dough to a lightly floured surface. Knead the dough for about 10-15 minutes until it becomes smooth and elastic. If the dough is too sticky, you can add a little more flour, but avoid adding too much.
3. Bulk fermentation:
    - Place the kneaded dough into a lightly oiled bowl, cover with a clean kitchen towel or plastic wrap, and let it ferment at room temperature for about 4-6 hours, or until it has doubled in size. During this time, perform a series of stretch and folds every 30 minutes for the first 2 hours.
4. Shape the dough:
    - Once the dough has doubled in size, gently deflate it and shape it into a round or oval loaf. You can incorporate raisins or chopped nuts into the dough during this step if desired.
5. Final proof:
    - Place the shaped dough on a piece of parchment paper and cover it loosely with the kitchen towel. Let it proof for another 1-2 hours, or until it has visibly expanded and feels airy to the touch.
6. Preheat the oven:
    - About 30 minutes before baking, preheat your oven to 450°F (230°C). Place a Dutch oven or baking pot with a lid inside the oven to preheat as well.
7. Score and bake:
    - Once the oven is fully preheated, score the top of the proofed dough with a sharp knife or bread lame to allow for expansion during baking.
    - Carefully transfer the dough (along with the parchment paper) into the preheated Dutch oven. Cover with the lid and bake for 20 minutes.

8. Remove the lid and bake:
    - After 20 minutes, remove the lid from the Dutch oven to allow the bread to brown and develop a crust. Bake for an additional 20-25 minutes, or until the bread is golden brown and sounds hollow when tapped on the bottom.
9. Cool and enjoy:
    - Transfer the Cinnamon Sourdough Bread to a wire rack and let it cool completely before slicing. Enjoy slices of this delicious bread on its own, toasted with butter, or as a complement to soups and salads.

This Cinnamon Sourdough Bread recipe yields a flavorful loaf with a subtle cinnamon aroma and a chewy texture that is characteristic of sourdough bread. It's a wonderful treat to bake at home and share with family and friends!